T0128290

NOT WITHOUT HOPE

Where Then Is My Hope?
JOB 17:15

The True Story of One Child's Journey from Tragic Losses to Healing

Judy Kimble Williams

WESTBOW
PRESS®
A DIVISION OF THOMAS NELSON
& ZONDERVAN

WestBow Press books may be ordered through booksellers or by contacting:

WestBow Press
A Division of Thomas Nelson & Zondervan
1663 Liberty Drive
Bloomington, IN 47403
www.westbowpress.com
844-714-3454

ISBN: 978-1-6642-9234-5 (sc)
ISBN: 978-1-6642-9235-2 (hc)
ISBN: 978-1-6642-9236-9 (e)

Library of Congress Control Number: 2023902870

Print information available on the last page.

WestBow Press rev. date: 03/09/2023

ACKNOWLEDGEMENTS

To Gene, my dear patient husband of 5-plus years who has shown me much unconditional love. Gene, your gentle demeanor and your heart of understanding have nourished my soul. I could never have finished my story without your listening ear and your words of comfort as I have continued my journey of healing, while writing. I am forever thankful for our relationship, a gift from our Lord.

To my children, Julie and Brad, you both were greatly lacking in the mothering that a child deserves. However, your own parenting skills amaze me. You make me proud! Thank you for showing me love and respect, and for giving me the greatest gift, my grandchildren.

To my sister, Linda Crock, we have basically traveled this journey together from babes. I can't imagine my life without you. Through laughter and through tears, you have been the one who could understand me like no other. Only in heaven will we understand more of the "Why" of it all.

To Joyce Lamphier, my friend whom God placed in my life when I was finally able to voice some of my untold story. In a booth at McDonald's, drinking coffee late into the evening, you, many times, listened as I tearfully shared with you some of the shameful, painful memories for the first time. You helped me piece together the "patchwork quilt" of my life, giving me my first solid picture of my life story. Your encouragement has been priceless as I handed you piece after piece of my rough writings for you to critique. Thank you for your loyal friendship these many years, and for working with me to the finish.

To my friend, Becky Hardesty, you, with your great organizational skills helped me sort out my journaling, going through countless pages to start me in the right direction when the seed to write my story began to germinate. Your enthusiasm fanned the small flame in my heart to get started. I am forever grateful.

To so many others who have been a part of my journey, I couldn't begin to list the many who have had an impact on my life. I thank you!

Our home. Circa. 1953

Our family.
Daddy (Marvin Kimble), Mother (Mary),
Jeanette, Jimmy, Barbara, Judy (me), Linda

Judy (me) circa. 1942

Barbara
Daddy positioned Barbara on a cushion on our
kitchen floor, capturing the sun rays coming
through the window. Circa. 1939.

Daddy, Mother, Jeanette, Jimmy,
Barbara (baby) circa. 1939

Mother, Daddy, Barbara, Judy,
Jimmy, Jeanette circa. 1941

CONTENTS

PART 1

Splashing, Music, and Carefree

"COME ON. PLEASE, JUST ONE MORE TIME. GET IN the tire. You won't go in the water this time, I promise."

These were the words of my big brother, probably eleven or twelve years of age, begging this little gullible child to curl herself up in the rubber tire to be rolled down the hill and into the creek again, or maybe he really was aiming for the little bridge crossing the creek, which we used when going from the house to the barn. No matter what his aim, I always ended up in the water, though not deep enough to drown me.

My story begins in rural West Virginia, eastern panhandle, in a little four-room house, in a valley between two West Virginia mountains. Everyone knows, if one is between two mountains, there is also a stream meandering through that valley. This wonderful stream running just beyond our yard was the favorite part of my childhood as my sisters, my

1

brother, and I spent many hours a day there, as soon as it was warm enough to bear the cold of the mountain water. Hot summer days found us three younger ones, Barbara, Linda, and myself, in our little dresses with dress tails tucked in our panties to prevent them from getting too wet, building a dam or else catching crabs (crayfish), tadpoles, and minnows, putting them in one of Mother's canning jars or in a can.

It was also in one of these dammed-up places, where the water would be a little deeper, that big brother Jimmy would go to the outdoor toilet, get a handful of toilet paper, if we were fortunate to have real toilet paper on hand, and use it to cover the mouths of his three little sisters as we had a baptismal service— Baptist style. We had no choice in the matter as he could outrun us. We usually did whatever he wanted as he could be pretty rough with us if we didn't. He had so wanted a baby brother when our little sister, Linda, was born, giving for him four sisters, one older and three younger than himself.

I was born in the fall of 1940, the fourth of five children. Firstborn sister, Jeanette, was nine years old when I was born, Jimmy was six, and Barbara was three. My little sister, Linda, was born in 1943. Our parents and grandparents had survived World War 1, the Great Depression, and our nation would be entering World War 2 shortly after I was born.

Mother was a wonderful person, always busy taking

care of her family, cooking on a wood-fired cookstove in the summer and winter, and doing laundry for this family of seven in a wringer washing machine with a gasoline-powered engine. We had no electricity nor running water, except for the fact that it was running water, as we would run from the well to the house with a bucket of water.

The wringer washer sat on a small open back porch. On a bench behind the washing machine sat two galvanized wash tubs in which to rinse the laundry. I'm sure it was a true labor of love for our mother to do that mountain of laundry every Monday with a washer that could be very stubborn about deciding whether it even wanted to start. I remember her using a blue liquid called "bluing" in the rinse water to make the "whites" whiter. On the kitchen table sat a large round aluminum dishpan of liquid starch, which, I think, she had to cook on the stove to make it. She dipped Daddy's shirts in this rather thick liquid to "starch" them and wrung them out by hand before hanging them on the clothesline. Our little Sunday dresses were also starched, hung out to dry, brought inside to be "sprinkled" with water, and rolled up in a wooden bushel basket along with all other items to be ironed. All our articles of clothing were placed tightly together for the moisture to permeate each piece. There were no cotton blends in those days, just cotton, and everything we wore had to be ironed.

Iron(s) were heated on the cookstove to begin the ironing process. Mother heated two of them, and using a removable handle, which could be transferred from one iron to the other, she used one until it became too cold to iron out the wrinkles then placed it back on the stove to heat while she used the other hot iron.

I remember once when I tried to "help" Mother get us ready for church. She had put a beautiful pink coat with satin lining, belonging to my little sister, on the ironing board. While she was doing something else, probably waiting for the iron to cool enough to use on this delicate fabric, I decided to iron Linda's coat myself. By the time Mother saw me, there was a brown scorched place in the shape of the iron on the little coat. She picked it up, looked at it, and laid it aside. She didn't scold me, but her disappointed look left me feeling so guilty. I hated disappointing my mother.

With no electricity and with just an eggbeater as a mixing tool, Mother often mixed up ingredients for cakes with her hand, allowing us smaller ones to lick the cake batter from her fingers after the cake was properly mixed. She baked bread often, and I remember once I got my hand smacked for sticking my finger down into the high mound of raised dough in the large aluminum dish pan.

Mother would also help out our neighbors with health issues as she was a nurse. She had met our daddy when she was a nurse in the hospital in Davis,

West Virginia. Daddy had fallen at the Fairfax Stone Plant near Davis and had broken his leg. I don't know the details, but this probably was her first and only job outside of being a wife and mother. I can just imagine how romantic their acquaintance and courtship must have been. Pictures of them when they were young showed their love for each other.

Life was simple. We children played outside when weather permitted. Daddy had put up a rope swing in a large maple tree where we could take turns swinging. It was across the creek we called the "run," far enough from the house so our voices wouldn't keep him awake when he slept in the daytime, preparing for his nighttime job at the Celanese Corp.

With the simplicity and innocence only a child can have, just being outside and loving nature was great for me. Lying down flat on the ground and looking up through the branches of a large tree or gathering soft green moss from the woods to "carpet" our playhouse, which consisted of a row of rocks for the walls and an opening in the rocks for our door into the playhouse, was a most awesome experience. The moss felt so good on our bare feet, soon toughened as we were allowed to play outside without our shoes from early summer until cooler weather came in the fall. Cuts and bruises and stubbed toes were all part of our summers.

Linda and me. Circa.1948

I loved crossing the dirt road just in front of our house and going a short distance into the woods to pick wildflowers and at times looking intently at the delicate design of the petals and other parts of a beautiful blossom. The mountain laurel was one of my favorite flowers as the bloom on those larger green bushes was so beautifully shaped.

We were taught to obey at a very young age. "You come when I call you!" was Mother's command, and we never asked, "What do you want?" We just went to her.

If we disobeyed, we knew we were going to get that little switch used on our legs. We knew not to run away from her as her words were "Don't run from me, or you will get it twice as hard when you come back."

Often Mother would make us go get the switch with which she would switch us. Yes, we tried to bring in just a little flimsy branch that would not hurt so much, but she just sent us back out to get a "better one." She was such a quiet, patient mother.

Music played a major part in our family, and I remember my mother having a song on her lips much of the time. Sometimes I would observe her singing a hymn as she worked, and then she would stop somewhere in the middle of the song. I had to become a mother before I realized the reason for this. I now smile at the thought. This child's mind believed if you start a song, you should finish it.

Through most all my years at home, the radio was our only outside source of entertainment, along with the wind-up Victrola, a record player that played the 78 rpm records. After we got electricity in our home, when I was ten years old, we were fortunate to have radio stations that played good quality music. We had no television until I was about sixteen years of age.

We had a piano which my parents were able to play, and Daddy played the guitar. Our entertainment was mostly the music we made as a family, with parents at the instruments and all of us singing.

We had a small battery radio, and on Saturday nights, whenever Daddy was at home, which wasn't often, he would like to listen to some country music program. However, the static was so bad, I found little joy from all that noise.

I remember once, in the middle of the day, Daddy was in the house teaching us a hymn from the hymn book titled *I Need Jesus*. He showed me the music notes, teaching me when to hold a certain note. A precious memory this became to me as having Daddy's attention and more importantly, the message of this hymn. God surely has brought the message of this song back to my mind, time after time, throughout my life.

Our dad worked night shift at his job, plus tending our small farm and his parents' larger farm adjoining ours with only one horse and a plow. He was a perfectionist of sorts in everything he did. But actually, now that I think about it, it was probably his perfectionist traits that made him a harsh disciplinarian. I should know as I followed in his footsteps.

He was a faithful husband and dad, taking every responsibility seriously. And two things I know for sure: he loved my mother, and he wanted to obey God. Many times I would come running into the house to ask Daddy something as he was getting ready to go to bed, and Mother would say, "Go upstairs and ask him. He's not asleep yet."

And as I would get to the top of the stairs and look into his bedroom, he would be on his knees praying. I would quietly wait until he finished praying to ask him my question or to tell him something. My little sister, Linda, remembers more of this than I do, and she says sometimes she would kneel beside Daddy as he prayed. Linda, being the youngest of five, naturally remembers more of the gentle love of our parents.

ooooo

In the few years before I was born, Daddy had worked diligently, building a house for us, which consisted of two rooms on the first floor and two bedrooms upstairs. Since the house was so small, the stairs leading to our bedrooms were very steep. Only my two elder siblings had been born at that time, but a third, fourth, and fifth would come along soon and make our bedroom a rather crowded one.

Daddy also built a two-story barn, along with a brooder house in which to keep the baby chicks warm that we received through the mail in large flat cardboard boxes with round one-inch holes in the sides. When the little chicks were big enough, they were moved to the upstairs of the big barn, where they provided eggs for us and eggs for Daddy to peddle from door to door in Cumberland, Maryland. The downstairs of the barn became a tool/machine shed.

Though we younger ones were not allowed into the brooder house, I would often sneak in behind Daddy when he went in to feed the little chicks. It was warm in there, and I loved the smell of the baby peeps. Daddy would sometimes allow me to hold one of the little soft lively balls of fluff.

Often Mother would have Daddy kill one of the chickens on a Saturday, and she would cook it so our Sunday dinner would be already prepared. She did not usually cook on Sunday unless we were having "company" for dinner. When that was the case, the adults ate first, and the children waited.

I idolized my daddy. There are no words to express my love and devotion to my dad. I longed for—intensely craved—attention from him. I so hungered for him to notice me, to give me a compliment, to simply acknowledge I was important. My little heart was screaming for attention from him. However, as he became busier, when he did notice me, it was usually to discipline me for something. I was so shy that I could not even answer him when he would try to correct my wrong behavior. At these times, he talked to me, but I didn't talk to him. I was afraid of him, and I was very stubborn.

A younger child soon learns what not to do by watching the elder siblings get into trouble. I didn't need much discipline. A stern look was enough to change my wrongdoing. I certainly didn't want Daddy doing to me what he did with my elder siblings. He beat my brother severely at times. It seemed he thought he could beat Jimmy into being an obedient young man.

Our church was within walking distance of our house, less than a half mile. Our parents were involved with activities there as Mother played the old pump organ and later the piano, and Daddy, for a time, was the Sunday school superintendent, though I do not remember much of this. I do remember him holding me on his lap twice, and those times were at church.

Daddy did the best he knew how with all the responsibilities he had. He was carrying a heavy load, and his losses were not few. For one, when he was a young adult, he had lost his eldest brother with appendicitis. Uncle Forrest left a wife and three children. They may have been living with my grandparents at the time. My grandparents kept the eldest child, Dennis, the only boy, and their mother took his two younger sisters and left the farm.

During the Great Depression, work had been sparse, and Daddy had searched different locations for work. They lived in different places, including Cumberland, Maryland, and I believe Daddy had even traveled to New York City to find work.

With God engineering their circumstances, they

finally ended up settling in the spot where I spent my childhood and close to the little church, which would be the life-building foundation of our young lives. Our little farm was down in the valley but also included property to the top of the mountain adjoining our grandparents' farm with a dirt road leading through the "sugar camp" to their house in a roundabout way.

Daddy had moved his growing family into an old log cabin, we referred to it as a barn, which belonged to a nearby neighbor, until he could get a house built for them to live in. Barbara was born in that old cabin. I am unsure of how long they lived there.

As times were difficult and the weight of World War 2 was heavy on everyone's heart, there seemed to be a special concern for one another's families. Daddy was a very thoughtful neighbor. Often, on his way to Cumberland, Maryland, to peddle eggs to customers, he would stop at our neighbors' houses along our road to see if they needed anything. One such family was the Bill Barnes family as Bill was away fighting in war for a time. He had a wife at home and two or three little children at that time. Also, neighbors brought their little boys to our house for Daddy to cut their hair. The barber chair consisted of our big metal sugar bucket placed on a kitchen chair. Daddy would lift each little one up on that perch and cut his hair.

A picture is worth a thousand words. Daddy loved taking pictures with his little box Kodak camera that held a roll of film for taking just eight pictures. He did candid shots of his family and of all the neighbors and their kids who came to our house. He was a very likable person, and all the neighbor kids loved the attention he gave them. For me, it seemed he gave the neighbor kids more attention than he did his own children.

Sundays, after coming home from church, while still in our "Sunday clothes," there were lots of snapshots taken. The pictures he took would be a tremendous blessing in later years as each of us have had to try to piece together the broken hearts that would be in the near future. I'm sure Daddy was very proud of his family. I'm sure he showed his pictures to many of the people to whom he sold eggs and thriving on their comments, like "Oh, what a beautiful family you have. My, you must be so proud of them," and I know, down deep in his heart, he was.

Daddy was very handsome and dressed very professionally, even to go peddle eggs. I went with him once that I can remember, and once again, I was very jealous of any customer taking up too much of his time.

My eldest sister, Jeanette, was always fun-loving. I remember her wanting to play, and it was difficult for Mother to keep her in the house to help with the work. Her relationship with our brother, three years younger than her, was always volatile. They fought much of the time.

Having Jeanette's approval was very important to me. As a small child, when I had questions about life, she was the one to whom I went for answers. At times we got along well, and she did like to have me with her, but she was also very jealous of me. She had developed a habit of pinching me right in the front of my throat, getting just a little piece of my skin every time our paths crossed in our very small house. And it hurt. But I would very obediently stop and let her pinch me. I actually would have a little callous on my throat where she pinched me time after time. Daddy sometimes saw her do this and would tell her to stop pinching, but it didn't stop. It is interesting, as I now think of these memories, and I wonder why I didn't kick her or try to protect myself. Actually, I really didn't think I had an option, and it was some attention given to me, and even if it did hurt, at least I was being touched. I have no memory of how old I was when this began nor how or when it ended. My sister, Linda, told me in later years she was jealous of Jeanette touching me.

I was also being sexually molested by a relative. My first memory was when I was approximately seven years old, but I know distinctly that this was not the first time this had happened. The molestation continued on for several years, and the guilt and shame I carried because of this has affected my sense of self-worth for much of my life.

Our parents taught us the difference between right and wrong. Mother corrected us when we used any slang words, like "heck" or "darn." These character traits were reinforced at school. Our reading books and the songs we learned in our morning opening were filled with honesty, being kind, having a good attitude, and patriotism, among others. We all stood, saluted our American flag, and recited the Pledge of Allegiance. I loved our morning music as our teachers would sometimes teach us new songs.

Once, when I was in first grade, I told my teacher I didn't have any lunch money, 10¢, as I had already planned to go to the store after lunch to spend my dime on candy. Some of the other kids had money to spend every day, and I didn't, or if their parents had an "account" at the little store on the corner in Fort Ashby, they were allowed to charge their sweet treats.

So I sat there at my desk as the other kids ate their lunches, waiting until we would be dismissed to the playground. Those with a couple of pennies would be allowed to go to the store, just one short block from our elementary school. That day I quickly got to the store, purchased two boxes of Luden's cough drops, 5¢ a box, and went back to my classroom without opening them. I could hide them in my desk, I thought. My mouth was watering for one of those drops.

My teacher, Mrs. Jenkins, saw me come back into the classroom and said to me, "I thought you didn't have any lunch money. Go back to the store, return them, and get your money back."

No smack on the hand with a ruler, no lecture about lying, just that statement. The humiliation of having to return them was enough. I was so glad most of the other kids were outside playing. I must say it was a good thing I got caught almost every time I was dishonest.

My memories of Barbara as a child were usually involved around music. She was the middle of five, but she was the eldest of us three younger ones and, therefore, was considered the "ringleader" when the three of us got in trouble. I remember a couple of occasions when I felt so guilty for her being the only one whose legs got switched for disobedience when I knew I was as guilty as she. But Mother's words to her were, "You are older, and you should have known better."

Linda and I followed her wherever she went, whether it was wandering too far from home as we followed the stream of water or just getting into something not allowed. She knew no fear, at least none of the things for which I was afraid. I was shy; she was bold. I was a people-pleaser; she didn't care, seemingly, what other people thought. One thing we had in common: We were little rebels. Hers was obvious, mine more subtle, but equally damaging to our lives.

Barbara loved playing the piano. She sang solos in church, and a few times, she and I sang duets. She played the piano at church sometimes on Wednesday nights when she was a teenager and probably other times. I remember one Wednesday night in the summertime, when she was playing the piano, a wasp had gotten under her dress and stung her several times on the legs. She never stopped playing the piano but finished playing for the service. As she showed me later the large welts from the stings, my heart hurt for her. I voiced my surprise that she didn't just get up and run out of there. I think I would have.

Barbara was much more fluent in expressing herself than I ever was. She was tremendously gifted in her verbal expression, which, at times, was a curse to her and often got her into trouble with her siblings.

OOOOO

Shortly after my baby sister, Linda, was born, our mother was diagnosed with "Bright's" disease, a kidney disease for which there was no cure. She was in and out of the hospital several times. These memories are sparse in my mind, but I remember her spending time on the couch with very painful headaches and Jeanette putting cold washcloths on her forehead.

I do have one memory of Daddy bringing her home from the hospital and she was lying on the couch when we came home from Grandma's house, where we had stayed while Daddy was gone. I remember her hands and how long her fingernails had grown. So according to this, she must have had a lengthy stay in the hospital at this time.

Mother's illness was taking its toll on our family. Jeanette, being the eldest, was given more household responsibilities, like cooking, and even when Daddy was home, his mind was elsewhere. I cannot imagine what must have gone through his mind as he worked night and day to keep up with all the responsibilities he felt he had to carry.

World War 2 was going on, and his baby brother, my uncle, Bud, along with his nephew, Denny, son of his eldest brother who had died, were overseas fighting. Young Denny was killed, and Uncle Bud returned home after the war was over. To say the least, life was difficult, and now his beautiful wife and mother of his five children would soon be gone.

One evening we were all at the kitchen table eating supper. Daddy was at one end of the table, and I was at the other. I looked up, and he was looking right at me. I smiled at him. There was no response from him. I was crushed. My little heart felt such rejection. Daddy didn't even notice me. It would be many years before I would realize why Daddy didn't see my smile meant just for him. His mind was far, far away.

As I now think about that most painful incident, I wonder how different my life would have been if Daddy had suddenly noticed the fallen look on my face and lovingly spoke, "Honey, I am so sorry! I didn't mean to ignore you," or something similar.

PART 2

Tragedies, Loss, Insecurity, and Anger

ONE DAY, AS I WAS SITTING IN MY THIRD-GRADE classroom, I heard the ambulance siren as it passed by our elementary school. My life as an eight-year-old was still quite carefree, and though the siren was rather unusual, it never occurred to me anyone I might know was about to be rushed to the hospital.

That afternoon my three siblings and I got off the school bus in front of our home. As we walked in the front door, my child's heart told me something just wasn't quite normal here today.

I saw our mother's friend, Marie, who was down on her hands and knees scrubbing our kitchen floor. Another dear friend and neighbor, Myrtle, had taken down the curtains that hung at our kitchen windows. Though there was a fire in Mother's wood-fired kitchen range and also a fire in our pot-bellied stove in the living room, our kitchen looked and felt very cold and foreboding without the curtains.

It truly is amazing what a child can observe in just a few seconds. What their maturity lacks, their unconscious sense of childish intuition can whisper, "Something is terribly wrong, and I am scared."

My mother and my little sister, Linda, who was too young to begin school, were also in the kitchen. To me, it was a somber sight. Everyone looked so serious.

Within a couple of minutes, someone had actually said out loud that our daddy had shot himself and was in the hospital. I felt very much afraid. In an instant, my fun-filled life was turned upside down. Indescribable shock and unbelief filled our home.

Our daddy passed away a few days later, never having regained consciousness. Mother was notified by her dear friend, Grace Funk, that Daddy had passed. Grace lived in Fort Ashby and had a telephone. She came to deliver the sad news. She knocked on the front door of our home in the wee hours of the morning of March 7, my mother's forty-first birthday. I was in bed with my mother. Without getting out of bed, she called down to Grace, "Come in."

Grace came upstairs to Mother's side of the bed and spoke, "I guess I don't need to tell you ..."

I remember very little of the days leading up to the day of the funeral, except that neighbors had brought an enormous amount of food into our house with a large coconut layer cake standing out in my mind.

In listening to someone talking, I discovered Daddy had come home from work that morning, put down his lunch bucket, and told Mother they had booby traps set for him at his work. He kissed Mother and Linda and said he was going down to the neighbor's. He got back into his Ford pickup truck and drove down the road about a mile or two from our house. He borrowed a gun from Bill Barnes, telling him he wanted to shoot a dog. He then drove back up the road and pulled off somewhere between the Barnes residence and our house and shot himself in the head.

I remember going to the funeral home and seeing Daddy lying in the casket. The room was small, just for family viewing. As I stood there looking over the edge of the casket, I looked for the bullet hole in his head. There was nothing visible. I remember someone holding me on their lap during the funeral. I think it was my aunt, my mother's sister. The fragrant smell of the flowers was sickening to me.

Linda told me in later years, when our fourteen-year-old brother, Jimmy, learned Daddy had died, she heard him as he went over behind the barn and wailed like a wounded animal.

In our later years, Jim and I were going through some old family pictures. He showed me one of his school pictures and said, "This is about the time Daddy started talking to me, and then he died."

What my brother was not able to verbalize was Daddy had not only died, but he also left him on purpose.

I hope I will be able to adequately describe some of the lasting effects of a suicide. Every life that ends in this manner leaves more emotional damage and produces so much more pain than a death under normal circumstances, with many unanswered questions. I hope to elaborate more on the ongoing consequences of our dad's fatal decision. This choice has changed the landscape of all future generations in our family.

In my opinion, suicide is, without a doubt, the worst sort of rejection a person can endure. I struggle attempting to put into words the shame, the guilt, the rejection, and the huge void left in one's soul when a loved one leaves us in this manner. ABANDONMENT. Are there words to describe the pain and emptiness?

One day, shortly after Daddy's funeral, I was walking among the large maple trees that divided our farm from my grandparents, which led up and around the hill to their house. This bottom land was known as "the sugar camp." As I walked, an almost audible voice whispered to me in my spirit, "If you had done one thing different, your daddy wouldn't have done that."

I stopped walking, and my young mind immediately went to work.

Just standing there in the dusty road from which Daddy had driven his pickup truck back and forth to Grandma's house, I thought, *If I had just stepped here instead of there*, moving my feet about in the dirt, *Daddy wouldn't have done that.* I carried that lie for forty years, telling no one.

My little sister, Linda, would be starting school in the fall and needed to receive her vaccination before beginning her first-grade year. As the health nurse came to the school to administer these vaccines, I was the one who had to take Linda to school with me and keep her with me in my third-grade classroom the entire day of school so she could get her vaccination. When it was her turn to go into the room adjoining my third-grade classroom, I was allowed to walk her there and watch the nurse make that awful scratching on her upper arm with the needle. Six-year-old Linda screamed, and I thought my chest would burst with pain as I fought back the tears.

That summer after Daddy's death was one of some amazing events. We children continued going to church. Mother joined us as her health permitted.

The electric company had been in the process of bringing electricity up our dirt road while Mother was still living. The poles were being set in the deep holes they dug, and Mother told us to stay away from the workers. We were to have electric lights within months of Mother's death.

Revival services were scheduled at our church for late August as had been done in previous years. Barbara and Linda and I walked to church, getting there early for the first night of meetings. They would last ten days or two weeks. We knew there would be special music, and we loved learning the choruses and new hymns the visiting evangelist would teach us. I also remember the evangelist bringing with him a couple of times a male quartet who would bring special music. My heart was always blessed by good music. The message from the hymns and choruses we learned brought much truth and comfort to me. As these songs contained much of Jesus's love for me, I absorbed the love and trust of Jesus, but my vision of God was distant, demanding, untrusting.

Our church building was small with kerosene-lit lights on each of the side walls and, I believe, a kerosene light hanging down from the ceiling in the center of the room. When the weather became cooler each year, the men would place an old pot-bellied stove back into the middle of the floor and reconnect the stove pipe to the hole in the wall where the stone chimney would carry the coal smoke up and away. But this was summertime, so the old stove was back against the wall to have a little more space for seating.

That first night, we arrived early, and I sat on the second seat back on the left side of the church. I remember sitting there next to the center aisle before church started. Looking up, I saw my pastor and the evangelist sitting on the platform just a few feet from me. They were talking with each other. My eyes became fixed on this new face, and I couldn't stop looking at him. This was very unusual for me as I was a little fearful of the men in our church, and I simply didn't like men, in general; but I sat and stared. He eventually noticed me and must have said something to my pastor about me watching him. The pastor glanced down at me and then continued on talking with the evangelist. I felt embarrassed. I have come to realize, even then, I was suffering greatly from the loss of my father and was looking for any good man's attention to help fill the void in my wounded heart.

That first night of revival, several young people went forward for salvation; one of them was my sister, Barbara. Upon arriving home, I announced, "Mother, I am going to wait until I'm older and understand it better to get saved."

I don't remember how she answered me, but I am

sure she was praying for her little stubborn, strong-willed daughter.

The next night, I sat in the same seat as before. I don't remember a thing the evangelist preached on, but when the invitation to be saved was given, the conviction and drawing of the Holy Spirit was so real and so powerful. I obeyed the Lord, went up on that little platform along with an elderly man, Mr. Dennison, and God saved me. I prayed the prayer to be saved, but I do believe I had already gotten saved as I had left my seat. I had no problem knowing I was a little sinner in need of salvation as I could say "bad words" and tell lies, along with my brother. There was no real emotion, but immediately, I had a desire to read the Bible. I had a little New Testament, and I started reading it every night. Oh, how I wanted to do right and please the Lord. The desire was there, but my little independent spirit was not going to change quickly.

A short time after this summer revival service was over, a baptismal service was scheduled for all those who had professed Jesus Christ as their personal savior. Our mother dressed Barbara and me in white dresses, and we were baptized in Patterson Creek, just a few miles from our home.

What thoughts went through my mother's mind as she prepared to leave her children? How does a mother help prepare her children to be left with no parents?

I believe we must have had the bravest, most focused mother on this earth. Although her life had been shattered and her heart broken beyond description, our mother lost no time setting to work to do what she could to make our lives a little more comfortable as she knew she would soon be taken away from us also.

As I reflect on this time frame, I am astounded at the grace and physical strength God measured out to my mother in that time span after Daddy's death. She accomplished much in those last few months of her days on this earth.

One of mother's first decisions, which must have been so excruciatingly painful, was to establish a plan to help protect our sister, Barbara, as she had already seen firsthand the abuse Barbara would have endured from Jeanette and Jim if she was left in our home. With the trauma in all our lives from Daddy's choice to leave us, there was more discord and anger than can be described. No one knew what to do with their deep pain and anger. So Barbara would have gotten the worst from the elder ones. It was arranged that a family in our church, who had a daughter about Barbara's age, would take her to live with them. This, of course, fractured our damaged family even more.

For the last couple of months of Mother's life, Barbara was allowed to visit back and forth from our home to what would be her future home, as well as other times throughout her teen years. Even as I write this, my heart breaks for my sister's compounded rejection. Barbara's survival from her difficult childhood became what many rejected people do, which is, "I'll reject you before you have a chance to reject me."

Though she married and was the mother of three children, she lived her life never ever believing anyone could love her. Satan had also convinced her even God couldn't love her. She stated this in her suicide note at age sixty-three.

Mother had another small room added on to the house with a basement under it. The rest of the house was up on posts, and the wind would blow under it, making it very difficult to keep warm in cold weather. That new room became our kitchen, and the little cellar would be a place to store our canned food, potatoes, apples, etc. She bought a few pieces of furniture to put in the room that had been her kitchen, and this became a parlor, though I'm sure she intended it to become another bedroom as the sofa was a sofa bed. She also had a closed-in back porch added on so Jeanette would have a roof over her head as she did the laundry.

In the mix of her plans to do what she could to

make our lives easier, she had fallen and injured her tailbone. Now living in constant pain, she had to sit on an inner tube her doctor had given her. On another occasion, she had been rendering lard in the oven in a large rather flat oblong pan. When she attempted to remove the pan from the oven, it tipped, and the hot grease spilled on both her hands. The burns were very serious, and more pain was added to her frail body. We four elder children were at school, but Linda was at home, and she remembers this incident. She said Mother did not cry or make any noise from the burns but quietly asked Linda to go outside and sit down. One can only imagine the pure torture in our mother's heart. Did she cry out to God, "Father, how much more?" Her pain and losses were totally indescribable. Was there a total submission of her will with Mother saying, "Father, your will be done. I am ready to go to heaven!"

I remember her coming home from Cumberland one evening after shopping for some of the furniture that would be placed in our new parlor. She had also bought us some new cereal bowls and a few other items. I remember wanting to eat out of one the bowls, but Mother said they had to be washed first. They didn't look dirty to me.

Later on, she was sitting at the kitchen table, itemizing the money she had spent. There was a discrepancy. After working and reworking the figures, carefully documenting the money she had spent, she could not account for $20. She put the papers away and said, "I've never lost sleep over money, and I'm not going to now." That statement made an impression on my young mind.

My maternal grandmother, Mother, Linda,
Me, cousins Gerry and young Brooke. 1949
My mother, still able to smile through
her indescribable pain.

A young single adult son of our neighbor's had become a great help to my mother after Daddy was gone. As Daddy had done for our neighbors, Earl Hinkle was now doing for my mother. He began stopping by occasionally to see if she needed anything. At times, he would take mother to doctor appointments, grocery shopping, etc. His family had a nice farm about four miles from our home. I knew very little about the Hinkle family as they did not go to our church. Earl worked at the same place where Daddy had worked and was a very responsible man. He was not afraid of hard work and loved farming. His desire, I believe, was that he would carry on with his parents' farm when they were gone. Little did he know he would play a much more important part in God's plan for his life.

Though not yet a Christian man, he was a good man. I have no way of knowing what drew him to begin courting my eldest sister. I only know, when he became my brother-in-law, he also became the glue that held our family together.

One Sunday evening in late October, when they took my mother to the hospital, just months after Daddy died, I sat on the floor of her bedroom that evening with my back to the wall. I watched my mother as someone was there assisting her. She had gently and quietly asked me to go outside with the other children, but I couldn't leave her side. I guess at this time someone had already gone to call for an ambulance to transport her to the hospital.

I can picture them bringing her down the steps on

the stretcher and carrying her out the front door. She was so small and frail, and I was not able to see her form at all as the stretcher was being carried much higher than my head. We didn't even get to say goodbye to our mother, but of course, not any one of us was able to face the fact that she wasn't coming home. We just watched in silence. Linda and I sat in the corner of the living room on the studio couch.

After the ambulance had driven away, I once again had that nauseating emptiness and felt so alone, even though our little living room was full of people; at least that's how I remember it being. Fear and insecurity overwhelmed me. I had heard a neighbor lady whisper to another person, "They won't bring her back alive."

My child's heart welled up with intense anger toward this woman who, to my knowledge, had never been in our house before. How dare she speak of such a thing? I'm now thinking, to hear the truth spoken aloud would mean I couldn't pretend Mother was going to be okay.

Linda and I had each other. Though I know my other siblings were around there, somewhere, Linda was the only one I remember. Very soon thereafter, and even before this time, I felt a great need to protect my little sister. The responsibility brought such a heavy load to my heart, along with fear that it would be my fault if she might be hurt in any way.

Mother died a few days later, shortly after my ninth birthday.

"Judy's mother died today," she whispered.

I was in the fourth grade, and we were at school. The children who lived close by the school were allowed to go home for lunch. It was while we were out on the playground after lunch that I found out my mother had died. One of the girls who went home for lunch had been told my mother had died, and I overheard her whisper the news to another classmate. I tried to think it wasn't true but suddenly felt alone and alienated from the other kids. I wanted someone to tell me it wasn't true. "Please, someone take me home," my heart cried.

But I stayed at school. I have always felt my fourth-grade teacher, Mrs. Spencer, might have known about the death of my mother that day as I remember she spent most of the afternoon, it seemed to me, at least, reading to the class. We were not required to do any more schoolwork for the remainder of the day. It was this dear teacher who had also taught us to memorize Psalm 23. I was never consciously aware of this scripture being of any particular comfort to my heart in the months and years to come, but unconsciously, these verses of truth simply built on the firm foundation which had begun very early in my life.

That afternoon Linda and I didn't get to go home,

actually. We were told we needed to get off the school bus with the Singhas children. It was at their house where we were "officially" given the news that our mother had died.

The afternoon sun was warm, and Linda and I, along with my friend and classmate, Nan, were out in their yard, playing. A short while later, her mom opened the screen door and called out to Linda and me, "Did you know your mother died today?"

I nodded yes and then looked down at Linda. She, with a questioning look in her eyes, was looking up at me. She had not known yet as there was no way I could have mouthed the words to her.

OOOOO

A cultural reminder here: These dear people had come through very difficult times, and it seemed no one had the ability to show much compassion for any loss or heartache. Nevertheless, the neighbors did show concern, and some of them were very ready to give a helping hand where needed. This dear mother of my friend and classmate was a lifelong friend of our family throughout her long life. Myrtle was born in 1915 and lived until 2017. At this time, she was a young mother with four children. Being one of the only women I knew who had her driver's license and a car, Myrtle, with a willing heart, stretched herself thin for our family and others who needed a helping hand. They were fortunate to have had her own mother and the children's grandmother, Mrs. Twigg, living with them. Grandma Twigg kept a sense of continuity in their home, allowing Myrtle to be available to help our family.

ooooo

Once again, I remember going to visit that small room at the funeral home just for family. I stood back against the wall, not wanting to go up to the casket to see my mother. A woman told me to go up and "get it over with." At least, no matter what her words were, that is what she seemed to be saying to me. I was just tall enough to look down into the casket. I looked at my mother and watched to see if she was breathing. I convinced myself she was, in fact, breathing, but I didn't say anything to anyone. And again, I experienced the nauseous feeling from the fragrance of the flower arrangements.

At Mother's funeral, they sang the hymn "Does Jesus Care?" I guess those words were supposed to be a comfort to our hearts, but all I could do for many years after that, when I heard that hymn, usually at church, was to break down in silent sobs. I must say, though, I am sure God used this great foundational truth to help us realize that, indeed, Jesus did and does care.

Does Jesus care when my heart is pained
Too deeply for mirth and song,
As the burdens press and the cares distress
And the way grows weary and long?

Does Jesus care when my way is dark
With a nameless dread and fear?
As the daylight fades into deep night shades,
Does he care enough to be near?

Does Jesus care when I've said goodbye
To the dearest on earth to me?
And my sad heart aches 'til it nearly breaks;
Is it ought to him? Does he see?

Oh yes, he cares, I know he cares!
His heart is touched with my grief.
When the days are weary
The long nights dreary,
I know my Savior cares.
—Frank E. Graeff

I do remember a bit of the long ride to Davis, West Virginia, after the funeral to place the body of mother next to our dad. I sat in the front seat of Earl's Buick, between Jeanette and Earl. I felt special. I believe my sisters, Barbara and Linda, and possibly my brother, Jimmy, were in the back seat. When we got to the cemetery on that crisp October day, I'm most certain none of us got out of the car for the graveside service; and while I could be wrong about this, I don't remember anyone getting out of the car.

I have since learned that the age of the child, when abandoned, has a great deal to do with how that child remembers and how she copes with the loss. For the older ones, the trauma was much more realistic. For Barbara and me, ages nine and twelve, the loss was more complex in that, so the experts say, we were mature enough to understand the loss but not emotionally able to process it. Therefore, we just internalized all the pain and felt we had to go on living, pretending all is okay. Actually, none of us were able to communicate in words what we were feeling, and there was no one available to help us face our losses. Linda was six years old.

On Linda's and my first day back to school after Mother's funeral, I brought her with me into my fourth-grade classroom as we rode the early bus, and there was no one in her classroom. The kids who had ridden that bus talked and played quietly as we waited for our teacher and the other buses to arrive and for the school day to begin. I sat in my seat very quietly, and Linda was sitting with me. She laid her head down in my lap and probably went to sleep. We had seats on which two children could sit side by side with the desk attached.) Neither of us could talk, for if we had, we would have begun crying. I quietly watched the other few children interacting with one another. Some of them had known of my mother's funeral and probably felt very sad for us. I had no way of knowing. I only know I felt empty and lost, and it was my deepest desire to try to protect my little sister.

Linda awoke, sat up, and immediately vomited on the floor of my fourth-grade classroom. When Linda's teacher arrived at the school and came into our room, she looked at the mess and asked, with what I perceived as a touch of impatience, "What did you have for breakfast?"

No one said anything as she cleaned up the mess. She then took Linda to her own first-grade classroom, just across the hall from mine.

OOOOO

Some very significant things occurred within that month between Mother's funeral and my sister's wedding.

One crisp, cold morning, probably just a day or two after Mother's funeral, I got out of bed at my grandparents' farmhouse, where we three younger ones had spent the night. I got dressed, ate breakfast, and left Grandma's to return alone back to our house, possibly a quarter mile away. I knew it was time for a

Christian radio broadcast, *Back to the Bible Broadcast*, from Lincoln, Nebraska, with Dr. Theodore Epp as the speaker. When I arrived at our house, I tried the door, but it was locked. However, I found a front window just to the right of our front door, which was not locked. It was low enough that I could raise the window and climb inside. I quickly turned on the radio to listen to the broadcast. With no fire in our old black pot-belly stove, the house was very cold, and the silence reminded me that Mother was not there. I do not know where my sister, Jeanette, or my brother, Jimmy, were at this time. Standing close to the little battery radio, which sat on Mother's small table in the living room, I was nurtured and comforted by the beautiful music I heard and by the kind, gentle voice of Dr. Epp, who gave the Bible message.

As soon as the program was over, I turned off the radio and climbed back out the window and returned to Grandma's house. I don't remember anyone missing me for that short time. At Grandma's, I felt so lost and insecure. And I was cold. It felt like the cold penetrated not only my flesh but also my entire being as I would quietly stand behind her wood-fired kitchen cookstove.

One evening, shortly after Mother's funeral, Jeanette was sitting up, waiting for Earl to come visit. She never wanted to be alone with him and would have me to stay up late at night to be there when he arrived from his three-to-eleven job. On this particular night, I remember sitting on the sofa with her. She had gotten a bottle of something and had written a suicide note. She told me to give the note to Earl when he came. She drank the stuff and laid down on the sofa with her head in my lap and went to sleep. Six-year-old Linda was sitting at the top of the stairs watching all this take place. Though I have no memories of what I did, Linda tells me she remembers me talking to Jeanette and saying, "Wake up! Wake up!" as I tried to revive her.

She said I would lift her limp arm and let it down. Jeanette was totally unconscious. Linda also said she had thought the phrase "passing out" was synonymous with "passing away."

When I heard Earl's car pull into our front yard, I rolled her off on the floor so I could meet him at the door. I met Earl at the front door and gave him the note. I have no memories of what happened after that.

The losses in our family were so profound and so close together that we simply couldn't begin to process the overwhelming feeling of emptiness, like there was no footing, no foundation in our lives. Suddenly, it was as if no one was in charge. I truly have no memory of how we functioned. Jimmy, having the logical thinking of a male, was taking care of outside chores, and I believe he did want to be a responsible young man. He and Mother had had a close relationship.

Not only had we experienced the tragic death of Daddy, but also Mother's fatal illness and ensuing demise, all within seven months of each other, and then my sister's attempted suicide and her marriage just one month after Mother's funeral. This brought a stranger into our home and, thus, another adjustment. Added to this, I had lost my brave sister, my playmate, Barbara, the one who would go ahead of me in the deeper places of our stream, searching out frogs that might be hiding under the tree roots that jutted out over the water. I was always so afraid there might be a snake in those dark places, but she knew no fear.

One other memory I remember packed into that month before my sister's wedding was that one evening Linda and I, ages six and nine, came home from school, and Jeanette discovered we had head lice. She sent my brother to the store, five miles away, on his bicycle to get some really smelly stuff to put on our heads to kill those pesky bugs. She then saturated our hair with the liquid, wrapped our heads in towels, and made us stay upstairs that evening during Earl's visit. She would rather have died than have him know about the head lice. When we were adults, Linda jokingly said we brought them home but didn't get to keep them.

Though Earl later became the most important element of security in our young lives, all of us, including Earl, would have a difficult time trying to adjust to such an enormous situation. I have had questions in my later life as I have tried to process all the tragedy and changes in our family. One question that comes to my mind is, why in the world would a young single man, twenty-six years of age, take on such a responsibility as this? A few things: Times were different then, most young people matured more quickly, and responsibility was normal. Also, Earl had the kind of perseverance built into his DNA that would give him the courage to "hang in there." I can only imagine the times he must have asked himself, "What in the world am I doing here?"

The most important reason for me now as I look back is that God, in his sovereignty, had placed Earl in our family. Though we had no idea at the time, God, as he has promised over and over in his Word, was protecting us, these fatherless children, by sending a source of stability and security. Earl didn't use alcohol, and he had nothing in common with those who did. Though most people in our community were gentle, law-abiding citizens, we had also seen firsthand the pain and heartache in families where the daddy drank.

One day, when Linda and I were home alone, we

decided to look at some family photos. Though I tried, there were times when I was not able to remember what my mother's face looked like. We got out the box of pictures, and sitting together in the small rocking chair Daddy had refurbished, we rocked and looked at and studied the faces of our parents. There was one eight-by-ten photo of our parents and a couple of my siblings. I went to Mother's sewing box and got out a straight pin. Getting seated once again beside Linda, I proceeded to scratch out daddy's eyes with the pin. I had no conscious rationale for doing this. Afterward, I felt guilty for ruining the picture.

The picture I damaged.

45

Earl and Jeanette made sure that first Christmas would be one to remember. It was indeed the most joyful, pleasant Christmas I ever remembered. Each of us received one very special gift that year. There was such a spirit of "feeling alive" and of sharing our toys with one another. Jimmy received a BB gun, for which he used the balls on the Christmas tree and our behinds as targets.

Earl always loved to decorate the house with wreaths and electric candles in the windows and pretty things on the walls. He also made sure we had a nice hand-cut Christmas tree in the living room.

Sometime the next year, Earl got laid off from his job. Money was tight, and our car had been repossessed. Earl somehow got a flatbed truck, which barely ran, and he and Jimmy began cutting trees for pulpwood. The logs were cut into five-foot lengths and loaded onto the truck manually, chained down and hauled to Luke, Maryland, to the West Virginia Pulp and Paper Company. This was in the early 1950s.

One memory that stands out in my mind during the years when we had very little was one of those sad Christmas mornings when there was a knock at our front door, and as someone answered it, there stood two men from the fire department with arms full of bags of groceries. Do you think I was excited? I certainly was not—I was humiliated and ashamed and embarrassed. How can such a little one feel such emotions? Linda recently shared with me she also had felt such humiliation. People were being kind to share with us, but it just brought such a feeling of shame to me—to us.

My spirit of rebellion was already brewing before Daddy died. I remembered clamming up when he tried to get me to apologize to one of my siblings, and he didn't know what to do about that. The few times he spanked me, it was almost always in anger. His harsh discipline crushed my spirit, and many times, as I ran outside to cry, I breathed these painful words through my tears, "I hate him." Of course, I didn't hate him, but this was the only way I knew to express my deep hurt.

Jeanette was my authority figure, and while I was never outwardly rebellious, I deeply resented anyone bossing me around. My very independent spirit placed a bull's eye target on my chest and on my back. These were the footholds Satan used to attack me again and again and, therefore, setting up major strongholds in this child's life. I do so remember vividly being attacked in my mind many times with evil thoughts, impure thoughts no child would have the ability to think of on her own. And I felt evil and sinful and guilty and dirty for such thoughts. Though I knew in my heart God had truly called me to himself and miraculously saved me, the pull toward evil was prominent. Satan was determined to destroy me, and there was no one for me to talk to about this warfare. Having no understanding of this, I simply thought I was one wicked child.

As a teenager, I so longed to be able to talk to Jeanette about things that troubled me, but the few times I did get up the courage to approach her with a problem, she just laughed at me. That hurt. She was not really making fun of me, but I believe she just felt embarrassed or didn't have the ability to understand my feelings. I am sure I would not have done nearly as well as she if I had been in her shoes. Still, that's just the way it was.

Even when I was a very young child, Jeanette was my hero, and I had always wanted her approval. However, after our parents were gone, I had no way of comprehending the fact she was also devastated when she was left alone with four younger siblings. Her method of dealing with this pain was to lash out her anger and control on us younger ones. Receiving a slap across my face occasionally for no reason hurt me deeply. And even as much as this hurt my heart, as a teenager, I remember telling my friend I would rather be slapped in the face than to be yelled at.

Having been born with such an independent spirit, I had closed my spirit to her and everyone else in my life. My trust was shattered, and in a very unconscious manner, I decided I would never allow anyone close to me to hurt me or abandon me ever again. However, this closed spirit does create its own set of problems.

In her own damaged way, Jeanette desperately wanted me to need her, but she was so unstable and I was so independent that the roles became reversed. In her suicidal state, my deep fear of losing her consumed me, and her dependence on me gave me a sort of power and importance, or maybe I should say a heavy responsibility for a young child.

After our parent's deaths, I felt more introverted and self-conscious. I never talked back to Jeanette or anyone else. My sisters and I tried not to do anything that would cause Jeanette to be upset with us. We just attempted to be very obedient and do as we were told, but we *were* children.

Well, to be honest, many times we "stumbled" into trouble but seldom was it outright defiance. Like the time Barbara, Linda, and I had started out going for a walk while picking berries along the way. As we continued on, we ended up walking to the top of the ridge close to the home of our friends, the Dennisons, turning left onto another road, and headed toward the Hinkle farm, Earl's homeplace. This was certainly not our destination. We didn't have a destination. We were simply walking, talking, and playing along the way.

Following the dirt road and before starting down over the mountain on our little trek, we passed a peach orchard, which was part of the Hinkle farm. At the bottom of this steep slope sat the Hinkle homeplace. We tried to be very quiet as we passed their house as I'm sure Jeanette would be very embarrassed if she knew Mrs. Hinkle should look out her front door and see us, her daughter-in-law's little sisters, three little berry-picking girls walking past. We continued walking up hills and down hills until we eventually came back onto the road leading to our house. We turned left again and ended up back home, and a surprise was awaiting our return. That surprise was Jeanette standing in the front yard with a switch in her hand. We three girls got our legs switched, but good! I never knew why she punished us. Was it because we had been gone for such a long time and she was panicked? Or was it because we had possibly embarrassed her to the neighbors?

Even though we were never close, Jeanette had the ability to control me long after I was a wife and mother. I never did learn to tell her "no" about anything until I was in my forties, and even then, I needed the help of my husband to help me see she only had control of me because I allowed it.

On very cool mornings, Linda and I would run outside to sit in the sun to get warm if there was no fire in the coal stove that sat in our living room. Our favorite spots were on the back porch steps or down the hill to the bridge as these two spots were the two places where one could feel the warmth of the sun first. This one morning we were on the porch. I sat down on the first step of our back porch leading out into the yard and laid my head down on the bare wooden porch floor, kind of twisting my body so I wasn't too uncomfortable. The morning sun, now high enough to peep into our valley, warmed our backs. Our cat, Kitty Puss, was also lying there, stretched out, with a couple of her kittens playing about. I felt so lonely and lost, missing my mother. As I looked into this mother cat's face, I found myself scooting my body up onto the porch facing her. I looked deep into her eyes and thought, *She's a mother.* I pulled her close to me and for just a little while, felt comforted by the warmth of her body.

If the sun was shining down on the bridge, Linda and I would go down there and lie down on the warm boards laid side by side and nailed to two logs that stretched from one side of the stream to the other. There we warmed ourselves in the morning sun. Sometimes we would cross the bridge to the grass on the other side and walk around, all hunched over, and pretended we were chickens, clucking and making chicken sounds the way we had watched the chickens do when they were enjoying the sunshine.

It was mornings such as these that it was much warmer outside than inside our house in the early fall and late spring because no one built a fire in the stove as it would make the house too hot for the remainder of the day.

Another time, when I was probably eleven or twelve years of age, I was feeling very ill with some kind of a stomachache. There was no one who really paid any attention to us younger ones, so I probably had not told anyone about how sick I felt. In looking for some relief, I went outside and laid down flat on the cold ground in an area, where we had some grass. It must have been early spring as the sun was warm, but the ground was cold, and actually, the cold ground felt so soothing to my body. It was times like that that I would have memories of my mother and long to feel her gentle hands on my forehead or touching me, but all other times there were no conscious thoughts of either of my parents.

On rainy days, we played in the upstairs of the barn, where the chickens had been. The nests were still there, and there was still some dried-up chicken droppings mingled with the wood shavings Daddy had always scattered on the floor, which kept the chickens dry. After the chickens had been sold, Earl, for a few years, had stored some bales of hay up there, and it was on those bales we played. It was peaceful and soothing to be able to remove ourselves from the turmoil of our home, where it seemed that every move we made was being scrutinized. There were very few times of peace in the house or any place where Jeanette could see us.

Once, on a very rainy day, I got a box of Swans Down chocolate cake flour (or mix) out of the cupboard. It wasn't sweet. We took it to the barn and ate all of it. We often ate baking supplies Jeanette thought was impossible for us to eat. For instance, she had purchased a box of many, probably sixteen, different little bottles of flavorings, lemon, strawberry, etc., from the traveling McNess salesman. They really did have a strong flavor, but we just kept tasting them and tasting them until we simply tasted them away. When Jeanette found the empty bottles tucked back in the box in which they were purchased, we couldn't convince her we had eaten them. I don't remember whether we got our bare legs switched that time. Most always Jeanette switched us for the most minor offences. She was simply taking her anger out on the little ones. This made us very hypervigilant, always on guard.

Barbara was at our home for only short periods at a time after Mother died.

Anytime she was back at our home for a while, she would spend much time at the piano as she, like me, had a deep love for music. She could play all day if she had been allowed, but either Jim or Jeanette would yell, "Get away from that piano!" every time she started playing.

I had read a story in one of my library books from school about a large family of rabbits. Each of the bunnies was assigned a specific job to do in and around the house, and one of them was to play the piano while the others worked. That seemed like such a pleasant idea to me. We were called "lazy" if we were not busy.

Barbara told Linda in later years the Seeders family, with whom she spent much of her teenage years, was good to her. As an adult, she didn't remember being at home at all after Mother died. Several years after Barbara passed, when my brother was in the hospital, I went to visit him. He was delirious with some kind of infection and was talking nonstop. Most of what he was saying didn't make sense, but once he said something about Barbara taking her life, and he added, "I think I had something to do with that."

Though he never did ask her forgiveness, I know he was tormented with guilt from his unloving ways.

OOOOO

Bedtime was often chaotic. When Barbara, Linda, and I were finally in bed, we would either be fighting or would start talking and giggling. A couple of times this went on for too long, so Jeanette sent Earl upstairs to quiet us. In his frustration, he would grab Barbara by the shoulders and shake her in anger. (I must remind myself everyone was reeling from the tremendous adjustment of our recent past.) She got it first as she was in the front of the bed and easy to reach, I would be in the middle, and Linda was against the wall. After that, we would usually quiet down, and the sadness of missing our mother would seem to fill the room. Mother had always prayed with us.

After we finally quieted down, six-year-old Linda would stick her little foot out from under the covers, place it against the wall, and proceed to rock the bed until she went to sleep. That was her way of comforting herself; Barbara and I didn't want rocked, and we would keep telling her to stop. I was always feeling so smothered in the middle of our straw tick mattress, which sank down in the middle. The reason we had a straw tick mattress was that when Mother was still living, Barbara or Jeanette had brought a friend home to spend the night with us, and Mother discovered bed bugs later. She hauled that mattress outside and lit a match to it; hence, we slept on straw for some time after that.

A precious, comforting memory for me is when we learned this little chorus at church about "belonging to Jesus" (1 Corinthians 6:19b, 20). The absolute tenderness and warmth God placed in my heart as I learned and digested the truth of this song is amazing to me, even today, and still brings tears to my eyes.

> Oh, I love to hear his voice,
> Saying, "You belong to me.

You are not your own,
With a price, you're bought,
And you're mine eternally."

And I love to hear him say,
"I have saved you by my grace."

And when I get to glory,
It will then be grander still,
For I shall see his face.
—Wendell P. Loveless

God spoke to me through this little chorus and reminded me ever so kindly, "You are *mine!*"

However, it would take years for this truth to reach my heart from my head.

OOOOO

After the electrical wiring in our house was complete, Earl and Jeanette went to Cumberland and purchased a new electric wringer washing machine, a refrigerator, and a kitchen range. This was exciting, and I can still smell the "newness" of the inside of that refrigerator. The old oak ice box was hauled out of the house and into the barn. However, on some nights, when I couldn't sleep, I would lie there and listen to the sound of the refrigerator running, and it was not a pleasant sound.

I was used to the quiet of the country at night, with nothing but the sounds of crickets, the deep croak of a bullfrog, or a hoot owl.

Nighttime was when the emptiness of my heart would seem to surface somewhat, though not consciously. At times there was an indescribable feeling causing me to be so restless for such a long time. Eventually, I would go into a deep sleep, only to awaken later, about to fall off the edge of the bed and not knowing if I was on the side or the foot of the bed. Our bedroom was pitch-black once the lights were turned out, and I had to feel my way around the parameter of the bed to find my pillow. This must have been after a mattress replaced our temporary straw tick.

On a lighter note, there were times when several of us would make our own music. One of us would get a comb and wrap it in waxed paper, and the rest of us would sing the music, and no one sang just the notes. We added in all the musical instruments we could imitate—tubas, trombones, etc.—bump, bump, bump, bump, bump—filling in the "accompaniment" with our harmonizing "voice instruments." After one song was finished, we younger ones would yell, "Me next! Me next!" as we took turns with the musical comb.

The waxed paper-wrapped comb, which tickled my

mouth when I pressed it to my lips to blow on it, gave the sound of a violin. My brother was almost always the one who got these episodes going. He was so full of music and had a great tenor voice. He harmonized well as did all of our family.

A wintertime memory comes to my mind: Once, when I had been left alone at home, I decided to go ice-skating since the run had frozen over. By this time, I was probably ten years old, and our parents were already gone. I dressed myself in my beautiful Easter dress, put on my rubber boots, and thought I would be an elegant ice-skater. I'm sure I must have had on my white Sunday shoes inside those boots.

I knew exactly where there was a nice wide area of ice, and I headed straight toward it. The ice was smooth, and I was having a wonderful time in my pretend world. Suddenly, the ice broke, and I fell into the shallow stream, soaking my lovely dress and filling my boots with water.

It was extremely cold, but it wasn't the cold that bothered me. I knew somehow I needed to get back to the house and get my dress dried and back into the closet before Jeanette came home. I quickly changed my clothes and was holding my silky dress close to the stove to dry. I held it too close—it scorched, and a large hole appeared outlined in burned brown.

The only thing I could think to do at this point was to hide the dress so the truth could never be found.

To this day, I don't remember what I did with it, and if Jeanette ever did find it, I was not confronted about my fun-filled-day-turned-disaster or the fate of that dress.

OOOOO

Our dirt road, which ran just about a hundred yards from our front door, had portions of smooth flat clay with stretches of layers of shale. Fortunately, there was a very nice flat spot where we girls could jump-rope right in front of our house. We also played hopscotch on that flat surface, where one of us would draw the squares in the smooth dirt with a firm stick. In many places, we also could run down the road with the soles of our bare feet smacking the smooth packed-down clay without worrying too much about stepping on a sharp rock or stubbing our toes on the layered shale, which arose abruptly in the road.

Once, I remember pushing a long sturdy stick down the road, running, when, suddenly, the stick struck a rock embedded in that nice smooth surface of the road. The end of the stick I was holding came to a very sudden stop, striking me a terrible blow right between my ribs. It knocked the breath out of me, and I felt like I was going to die from the pain. I didn't tell anyone, but never again did I attempt to push a stick in front of me down the road.

We were allowed to go to the neighbors to play occasionally. We could walk down the road about a mile and play with the Barnes children. I will always remember her mom's lemon pies. On one of those playtimes, we must have gone to visit them on an Easter Sunday because even today at Easter time, I think of daffodils and lemon pie at their home. Mrs. Barnes was a kind, gentle lady.

I remember one evening we were allowed to walk about two miles up our dirt road to the Dennison home to play with Elva Jane and Judy. My brother, Jimmy, was also with us as they had a brother his age. It is possible, with Jimmy with us, that we were foolish enough to wait until dark to leave to go home. However, big brave brother was no help when we were so scared running toward home on that dark night. He outran all of us to our house. Left in the dust, I just knew a sleek black panther was close on my heels. Oh, such fear—the lights of home never looked so good!

This was one of the few times, after our parents were gone, when we were not given a curfew for whatever reason that I felt that no one cared about me. This is proof that children need boundaries to feel secure.

How can one put into words the emptiness of heart and home, the cold lonely places where just a few short months before, there had been warmth and security and love?

With Daddy working night shift when he was alive, we had been trained to stop and get very quiet if we had been outside playing or working or whatever before entering the house as Daddy may be asleep. I found myself still doing this after he was gone, forgetting he was not home and would never be there ever again. The shock to my emotions never ceased to surprise me. It was always the same letdown, sad feeling. Times like that were when reality would hit my heart for just seconds, and then the shell of protection had to be pulled back into place so I wouldn't have to feel the pain.

The one emotion I felt was anger. It always seemed to be brewing just beneath the surface, and when it did come out, it consumed me, like on that cold October evening, shortly after Mother's funeral, with a cold wind blowing through my coat, when Jimmy and Linda and I were outside, carrying firewood from the woodpile into the house. Linda had made me mad, and I threw a stick of wood and hit her on the leg. She cried, and I know it did hurt her. Jimmy picked me up and spanked me soundly just using his hand. He was only fifteen years old, but he never knew the profound impact that spanking had on my life.

Another time my temper got the best of me. Once, on my hands and knees, I was scrubbing the kitchen floor using an abrasive cleaner to remove black smudges from someone's shoes. I had to do everything as perfectly as possible. I could not put floor wax overtop any dirt. Jimmy came trudging into the kitchen in his dirty shoes and walked across my wet floor. I picked up the scouring powder can and threw it at him. I hit him a good one. Well, that was the second time my brother, just six years older than me, spanked my bottom. I don't remember any words of anger coming from my brother either time he spanked me, though there might have been. He also was carrying an enormous amount of anger and pain. I only know God led him and controlled him those two times to "provide" for me the appropriate discipline I needed, though that was just a small taste of what I needed to control this determined, rebellious spirit within me.

I believe with all my heart these two incidents stand out in my mind so profoundly because this would have been the role of my daddy. And he had left me. My concept of Daddy was that there was not one thing on this earth, not just in my own personal life, but even the unjust things that went on in the world that he could not fix and make everything work out just perfectly.

My teen years were tumultuous times for me emotionally. At school or at church, I attempted to be like other kids, but hiding my feelings of guilt, shame, and inferiority was very draining.

I do remember, several times during my teen years, of standing at the kitchen table after supper, facing two large round aluminum dishpans of water, one with hot soapy water for washing dishes and a pan of hot clean water for rinsing. Those times when I was doing that chore alone, which wasn't often, with an empty longing in my heart, I would look out our kitchen window that faced down the dirt road. It seemed I might be looking for any signs of life or activity, and I would think, *I wish someone would die.* Now, in reality, I certainly did not want anyone to die. I *unconsciously* was wanting something to happen for me to feel something, any kind of emotion.

I loved it when we had a downpouring of rain, causing flooding—I loved storms. I now believe it was because something was happening that caused me to feel alive. It didn't matter to me if it washed out the little bridge necessary for us to cross the run leading to the barn. It was just so exciting to get out of the house after the rain had stopped and stand or walk along the creek's edge, looking at the high water. I was very fearful of the deep, swift water swirling along, so I stayed a safe distance from the edge of the bank. We would walk a mile or two down the dirt road to see the damage done to the road and culverts along the way. But most other times I felt like a dead person inside.

Approximately halfway through my sixth grade, Jeanette gave birth to their only child, Marvin, named after our daddy. This new beautiful baby boy in our home was such a joyful event for us.

Much of the fear that had consumed me up to this time of my life—that is, of Jeanette possibly taking her life while I was at school—had diminished as it seemed, when she was pregnant, she finally had something to live for.

I was always terrified she would die, and I did everything that a ten- or eleven-year-old might do to prevent such a tragedy. I hid everything I could find in the house that seemed she could swallow to end her life.

As I look back on this, I now realize, since the devil had fed me his deliberate lie, "If you had done one thing different, your daddy wouldn't have done that," that to have been burdened down with being responsible for my eldest sister's death would have been unbearable. As one could imagine, I had become a control freak. I thought, if I could control everything around me, bad things wouldn't happen.

As Jeanette's emotional state improved, she and Earl made flower beds and grew beautiful flowers. She was also learning to cook and bake bread. Years later, she baked all kinds of pies and cakes—good memories for me.

ooooo

Going into seventh grade was a tremendous adjustment for me. Our class was transferred from a little cement block building, where we had spent our fifth and sixth grades, into the high school building containing seventh through twelfth grades. I was extremely shy and very fearful of this new environment. This entire year seems to have been an emotional nightmare.

My only salvation in seventh grade was my adult friend, Audrey Barnes. She was a single lady and the midwife in our area, whose house was within walking distance of our high school. Often I would get off the school bus at our high school building and walk to her house. She always welcomed me and seemed to enjoy my visits. I had a little window of free time from the time we arrived at school until our first class started as we rode the first run of a two-run bus schedule.

I seemed to be always hungry, and Audrey would often feed me something. She certainly did meet a deep need in my attention-starved heart, and she truly listened to me as I talked to her about my burdens.

Occasionally, Audrey would ask me to babysit for her for an entire day as she needed to go to work for somebody. She was rearing her sister's little girl and couldn't take her when she went to assist in the delivery of a baby. I remember one evening Audrey was very late getting home and I needed to prepare supper for us, so I decided to make potato soup. It was so thick that I could hardly get it out of the pan. Patsy and I had eaten some of it, and when Audrey came home, she looked at it but did not say one word of criticism to me.

Another time, when I had kept little Patsy for her, she wrote my excuse for school for being absent so Jeanette wouldn't find out about me skipping school. Jeanette had always signed my excuses with "Mrs. Earl Hinkle," but Audrey had signed it "Jeanette Hinkle." The next day, when I took the note to my homeroom teacher, Mr. Thomas Small, he looked at it and said, "Are you Jeanette Kimble's sister?"

Supposing I had been caught skipping school, I shyly said, "Yes."

Mr. Small had taught Jeanette in high school and must have known our parents had died. I believe that that note probably prevented me from failing seventh grade as he had mercy on me.

Another newfound escape I discovered, besides going to see Audrey—and sometimes skipping school—was books. I had developed a love for reading in elementary school and read all through my high school years. I consumed every mystery book in the school library, having gotten my reading appetite whetted by the gentle librarian, who suggested I read *Heidi*. I looked at that thick book and thought, *I'll never get that book finished*. I usually chose smaller books, but I obediently took her suggestion. It was such an adventure, and I was hooked. My "book escape" took me to many lands, studying how Indians and Eskimos lived and how their children played and worked. Adventure after adventure activated my vivid imagination to "see" things no social media could ever compare.

Jeanette seemed unable to function well at home with her new role of mommy and do the laundry as we still had no indoor plumbing and, therefore, needing to carry all that water from the well. So for most of my seventh grade, she would keep me out of school on Mondays, with the excuse written, "Please excuse Judy as she was needed at home."

The one negative thing that topped the long list of validating my feelings of worthlessness was the two male classmates who made my life unbearable at school. I know this probably wasn't for the entire four years of high school and maybe only in the ninth grade, but the damage done was to stay with me for many years. I felt like a wounded animal in a cage with people on the outside poking me with sharp sticks and me not being able to get away from them.

Struggling to keep my emotions under control, I mostly remained withdrawn and quiet, but I was truly a fighter, and eventually, I would say or do something extremely impulsive, like a volcano.

One little incident, which now brings a smile to my face, occurred when I was in the ninth or tenth grade. We were sitting in our classroom, in alphabetical order, which put "Mark" directly behind me. Well, as usual, "Mark" and "Fred" were tormenting me, and "Mark" hit me on the head, knocking the hair barrette out of my long heavy head of hair. I was very humiliated as my hair fell down over my face, and this was the last straw. I swung around and slapped his face with a terrible force. He and I were so shocked. He looked up at the teacher as if to say, "What are you going to do about that?"

He looked at Mark and said, "Good enough for you."

I do believe he backed off a bit on his bullying after that.

Sometime during my teen years, my brother, Jim, got married. He and his young bride lived with us for a short time. Eventually, they were able to purchase a small mobile home.

When I was sixteen, I went to take my driving test to get my driver's license, only to find out I was walking around nearly blind as I failed the eye exam. I was very nearsighted. I am sure most of the students thought I was very unfriendly as we walked down the hallway, changing classes, but I just couldn't tell who they were until they were quite close. Of course, this was normal to me, and I wondered how my friends walking with me could yell at a friend away down the hall and know who they were talking to. And yes, I did get glasses, only to find out later our church had paid for them—another blow to my ego, more humiliation.

I do believe, if there were just one positive highlight in my teen years, it would have been the month I spent with my uncle Brooke and aunt Peggy in Pittsburgh, Pennsylvania, along with my six cousins. This took place the summer between my sophomore and junior years of high school. Young Brooke was their eldest and Gerry was next. With four younger siblings, Gerry also had a lot of responsibility at home as her mom worked to help survive those difficult times.

Aunt Peggy had bought me a beautiful navy blue skirt for school. It was very neat and dressy. I loved it—I wore it and wore it and wore it! She also bought me a really cute modest swimsuit and would allow Gerry and me to ride the incline up to the public swimming pool. Such freedom I had never known! We were allowed to ride the streetcar to Kennywood Amusement Park all by ourselves. I felt somewhat uncertain about being able to do this, but Gerry was very confident, so I decided to just enjoy the day. Her younger sister, Gail, was too young to go with us.

With my aunt Peggy already having such a large family to feed and clothe, she certainly must have sacrificed a little bit more to see I had a memorable time at their house that summer.

When the time came to return home before school started, I simply dreaded going back home. I didn't realize why this was such a special month of my life until many years later. It occurred to me this was a time I had felt absolutely no responsibility for anything—I could just be a carefree teenager.

My favorite classes in high school were typing, bookkeeping, and office practice, all necessary for secretarial work. God had his sovereign hand on me. Though I didn't feel very close to him at all, he was engineering circumstances in a miraculous way.

That next summer I spent the entire three months living in Falls Church, Virginia, with a family who needed help with their two small children as the health of their mother was not good. This was the Bucklew family. This information had come to me through my sister, Barbara, who had been working as a nanny to the children of another family in the area. When I was to return home to finish my senior year in high school, Mr. and Mrs. Bucklew told me I was welcome to live with them if I ever wanted to come back to Virginia to get a job.

For me, high school graduation was a milestone for which I felt only relief. I was enormously happy to be out of school and never looked back. Another disappointment in my life was my graduation night with none of my family there for me because the brother of Jim's wife had been killed in a car accident earlier that day. Though very unconsciously, I buried my pain and never allowed myself to feel the burning disappointment of this loss until much later in life, but I felt so alone and insecure that night, even though I was among my classmates. It seemed they all had their family with them.

I left home just after graduation and returned to the Bucklew family in Falls Church, Virginia. I would live with them for the next two years. It was all a mixture of excitement, fear, and apprehension. I got an office job in Falls Church just two weeks after my high school graduation.

One of the many problems a child who grows up with childhood losses faces is they do not realize what they missed. To them, their life seems normal, and they feel they should already be equipped to face life in the work-a-day world. At age seventeen and coming from my home with no indoor plumbing nor a telephone, I definitely was a "country kid." However, I was full of myself, being very immature and very proud of being able to get a job so quickly. My overconfident exterior was a cover-up for my extreme feelings of inferiority. I was in no way ready to be thrust into this worldly atmosphere. It's so easy now to look back and see how a young innocent woman can be swamped and deceived by this drastic adjustment with very little accountability to anyone. I loved the freedom I felt of finally being away from home and not under Jeanette's scrutiny all the time. I was young and foolish. My great protection was I was very fearful of dating, of actually going somewhere with a guy in a car alone, so Jeanette's warnings about dating were not wasted. Along with her strict control of Linda and me when we were teenagers was this very wise advice, "The further you let a boy go with you, the less he will respect you."

Besides that, being so self-conscious, I had no idea of how to carry on a conversation with someone of the opposite sex. It had been my experience that most boys and men were not to be trusted.

I muddled through the necessary activities of going to work and coming home to spend all my free time with the Bucklew family. However, for the first six months, intense fear and feelings of panic would continue to race through my being each morning as we drove through the security gate at work.

I became friends with a girl my age, Mary, who had

come to work in the same office as I. She had a car. They had moved to Northern Virginia from Detroit, Michigan. She was as comfortable in city life as I was insecure. A short time later, another girl, Barbara, came to work at Melpar. I later discovered she lived just about four blocks from the Bucklew residence. She often invited me to her house. Her mother was good to me. It's interesting that the very first time I spent the evening with her, I attempted to clean her mother's gas range as her parents had gone out for a meeting. After what seemed a couple of hours, Barbara finally got me away from that project. Somehow I have always felt more comfortable in a kitchen than anywhere else. Many times I have overstepped my bounds by cleaning or insisting on "helping" another woman with the cooking in her very own kitchen. I will never quite understand the "why" of it all. Possibly that was the only thing I thought I could do well.

One Sunday afternoon, Mary and I went canoeing at a stream/waterfalls somewhere in Falls Church. When I returned to the Bucklew home, I told them casually we had gone canoeing. Mr. Bucklew asked me if I could swim. I said, "No."

He became very upset, yelling at me. The loud words didn't upset me. Instead, I suddenly had the warm feeling someone cared enough about me to think that I had put myself in danger. He actually showed concern I might have drowned.

Being a very moody and sometimes withdrawn young woman, I will always wonder how the Bucklews ever put up with me. But they were always kind to me, never being controlling but gently giving advice where they felt they should. It felt good to be treated like an adult.

I remember sitting on the brick steps of their home leading up to their front door that first fall, staring into space, my mind not really thinking, and not consciously realizing why I felt so alone. Years later, I thought it was probably that I missed my mother. She had died in October. The fall season was always more depressing to me than other seasons of the year.

For Christmas that first year in their home, 1958, Mr. And Mrs. Bucklew bought me my first Bible. I was so pleased. It was white leather. I began reading my new Bible every night, and it seemed, other than reading the Psalms, God kept bringing me back to the book of James. It is a rich book. I read it over and over. Several teachings of truth were prominent to me, but the verses that kept popping out at me were James 1:5–6 (NKJV), which reads, "If any of you lacks wisdom, let him ask of God, who gives to all liberally and without reproach, and it will be given to him. But let him ask in faith with no doubting, for he who doubts is like a wave of the sea driven and tossed by the wind."

I pondered these truths often and tried to picture

what this meant. I didn't want to be unstable as the waves of the sea, but I knew I was. I knew for certain God was prompting me to begin asking him for wisdom. The conditions for receiving his wisdom just seemed so out of reach for me, too deep. Still, it became my constant prayer for him to give me wisdom.

Living in the home of the Bucklews the first two years of being away home was certainly a wonderful gift from God to protect me in the suburbs of Washington DC. There was a routine in their home, and I learned something about the life of a normal functioning family.

When I would travel home on weekends, usually riding the Greyhound bus, my sister and brother-in-law would meet me at the bus station in Romney, West Virginia, which was about fifteen miles from our home. I soon found it didn't matter whether I was in Virginia or at home, I just didn't feel I belonged to either place. At home, Jeanette would criticize me. She told me, "That place is ruining you."

It would take me many years to finally understand that my sister was watching me do the things she had wanted to do but never had the opportunity. Daddy had bought her a typewriter before he died, when she was in the eleventh grade, and her dreams were big, I'm sure. However, her jealousy of me made us miserable. Looking back, I do realize I had always expected more from Jeanette than she was able to give.

At work, I excelled with my job and received several promotions. Putting on a good front, I tried to act as normal as others working there. However, always being too sensitive, it was very difficult for me to take even constructive criticism. If another older female worker criticized me, I just fought back the tears until I could be alone to cry.

Truths about right and wrong had been instilled in me from the time I had been a child. What a blessed gift this instruction was to me when I was suddenly thrust into the workplace.

I eventually found a Baptist church nearby and started attending. I loved going to the young adults Sunday school class. Our teacher, Mrs. Mills, was a mother of six children, and she had a great sense of humor, making her class feel welcome and not so self-conscious. She was such a good teacher, and I was hungry to learn.

I met Sonja Huddleston there, and we became friends. I discovered she was living with her married sister and that she was looking to get an apartment. I had been living with the Bucklew family for about two years, and it seemed natural that it was time for a move. Sonja and I decided to get an apartment together. These were fun years. It gave me a great sense of independence and taking on adult responsibilities.

Cooperating on sharing rent and food expenses worked out great. I loved to cook, so with me getting home from work each day much earlier than Sonja, I had time to fix meals. We were within walking distance of most stores and places of business. This was good as neither of us had a car.

Shortly after moving into our little apartment, I met a young man, Joe, who worked in an office adjacent to mine. He was working days there and attended college classes in the evenings. Joe became my ride to work each day as I always had a difficult time catching a bus. As we spent more time together, I began to realize he was about everything I had ever dreamed of in a husband. He was very kind, considerate, and always treated me with the greatest respect. However, he was also of another religious faith and not Christian. After discussing this lack of compatibility, I began to realize this was not the type of marriage I wanted nor would God want me to marry him because of the conflict this would cause in a marriage.

I prayed to God, asking his guidance but not wanting to have to make such a decision, knowing it would be necessary for us to stop seeing each other. However, I already knew the answer God would impress upon my heart before I asked.

After Joe left to go to his home in Texas for the Christmas holidays, I knew I would have to meet with him as soon as he got back. He came to my apartment to get me, and we went for a ride. With aching heart, I again asked him if he would begin going to my church, and I encouraged him to talk with his parents/family about it. He said, "What's the use of asking them if I already know what they would say?"

At the end of the conversation, I simply explained I couldn't see him anymore. Here I was, walking away from the only man who had ever treated me with such kindness and thoughtfulness. He was the only man who had ever sent me flowers on my birthday. He did love me, and I loved him.

I walked slowly from the parking lot and up the long sidewalk to my apartment; my feelings, a mixture of stubbornness, hurt, anger, and disappointment, overwhelming me. "What did I just do?" I asked myself. "How did I do that? Where did I receive the courage to take such drastic steps to end this wonderful courtship? I love him, and my heart is breaking. How will I ever be able to see him every day at work and still get over this broken heart?"

I did return to work, and indeed, I did see him every day, and the pain was unbearable. I fought back the tears at work as thoughts of the breakup went through my mind, and upon returning to my apartment each evening, the torrent of grieving broke loose, like a dam bursting. I lay across my bed, weeping and crying out my pain to the Lord. It was good I had time to be alone in the evenings. This was a godsend for me to have the time and opportunity to grieve this loss in private.

Several days went by, and the pain of my broken heart was not getting any better. I called my pastor. He agreed to meet with me that next Sunday after church services. As we walked into his office, he directed me to have a seat. I poured out my heart to him, and he listened. He then quoted Proverbs 3:5–6 to me and told me this was what I needed to do: "Trust in the Lord with all your heart, and lean not on your own understanding; In all your ways acknowledge Him and He shall direct your paths" (NKJV). I told him I would do that. He prayed with me, and I went home.

Still grieving at work and still fighting back the tears often throughout the day, I continued coming home, lying on my bed and crying out my pain to the Lord.

God was doing the healing, but I just couldn't tell it was happening. My heart was still too tender to tell it was mending. So, I once again called my pastor. He reminded me again to trust God with *all* my heart, in *all* my ways I was to acknowledge him, and he *would direct my paths*.

I consciously worked at attempting to apply this truth to every aspect of my life. Though my efforts were feeble, God, true to his promise, did bring wonderful healing to my heart, at least for this one particular loss.

I instinctively knew it was not in my own strength that I was able to be forthright and honest with this man and to have the courage to end the relationship. It was totally God, my Heavenly Father. He had the best plan for my future. For the first time in my life, I faced this painful event and experienced true emotions in grieving a loss and allowing healing to take place. I still have the letter of encouragement my pastor's wife, Hazel Wolford, sent me after I had made this decision.

Though I didn't consciously think about it, I believe I learned much from this experience. It was the beginning of realizing that God was indeed actively involved in my life. He had done what he promised he would do if I would surrender my desires to him.

I also found, when I *chose* to obey his principles, that of not marrying an unsaved man, he would empower me with his Holy Spirit to carry out the steps necessary to obey, no matter what my emotions were telling me. However, applying this truth in other aspects of my life seemed to be sparse. I lived and made most decisions based on my very unstable emotions for much of my life.

Less than a year later, God graciously sent me the man who would be my husband, a dream come true.

OOOOO

Philip Shrout came into my life after I found out

from a coworker there was a man who lived in his apartment building who had West Virginia license plates on his car. As I was looking for a ride home on weekends, I asked him if he would find out where this man was from in West Virginia. Long story short, that following Friday evening, Phil stopped by my apartment to pick me up. I was very thankful that he traveled through Romney, West Virginia, on his way to Parsons, West Virginia, where his family lived. My sister met me in Romney, and Phil went on to his home. On Sunday evenings, we met once again in Romney for our return trip back to Virginia. He transported, as well, a couple of his friends from Parsons who had gotten jobs in DC, so we weren't required to have to try to carry on a conversation. This was comfortable for us. However, after a few weeks passed, Phil asked if he could come over to my apartment and bring some of his music records. Of course, I said, "Yes."

One Friday evening, Phil came to pick me up at my apartment. We then traveled a short distance to the 7-Corners Mall parking lot to await the arrival of his friends who also rode home to West Virginia with him.

As we sat there chatting, he reached over into the glove compartment of his car and pulled out a small box. He opened it to reveal a complete set of very inexpensive wedding rings, his and hers. He quickly said, "These are from my first marriage."

Well, I'm sure the expression on my face gave away my feelings of astonishment and disappointment. It was at this very moment I realized I was in love with this man. My disappointment came because it was not in my plans to marry a man who had been divorced.

Watching my face to see my response, he broke into gales of laughter, so satisfied with himself that he had really surprised his little female friend. He said, "No. I found these."

I was so relieved, now knowing Phil was the man whom God had so graciously brought into my life. We married in August 1963.

Phil was everything I had always longed for, and my love-starved heart relished in his tender affection. His words were affirming. He was more able to express his love for me than I was to him. He never, ever, raised his voice to me. I certainly did get reprimanded a few times by him, and when this happened, I knew I had pushed him too far.

We settled in with the simple life of work, home, church, going to do laundry, etc. Though I was always happiest when Phil and I were together, there was very little real verbal communication between us as sharing our hopes and dreams, our failures, our fears.

After his discharge from the navy, he had been employed at National Airport in Washington DC, and that is where he worked when we first met. However, a couple of months before we were married, he was laid off from that job. He acquired another job shortly after that with Virginia Electric and Power Company. This would be the job which would allow us to move back to West Virginia, where he longed to be. So about two years into our marriage, Phil was notified he was to be transferred to the new Mt. Storm Power Plant in Mount Storm, West Virginia. He was excited to be leaving the fast pace of the city, and I was ready to quit my job as I was three months pregnant and very hormonal, not to mention the awful morning sickness.

I had no idea how traumatic this move would be for me—we moved to the dead little coal-mining town of Davis, West Virginia, in March 1965. The change in the climate was enough for one to have to adjust, and we were in no way ready for all this move would entail. I was later told that 1965 was one of the coldest winters there on record.

We moved into an old two-story house in Davis, and Phil began his new job. He was in charge of setting up the storeroom for this new power plant, and the long days he worked took its toll on me. He was working seven twelve-hour days. This left me at "home," if one could call it a home, and my neat little world began falling apart. For one thing, this house was very cold. I felt cold and lonely and very insecure in this new world of a ghost town.

I had gone from the city, working with people all day and coming home to a loving husband in a warm apartment, to being alone all day in a cold house where the frost gathered thick on the *inside* of my kitchen windows. I felt like I was living in an igloo. Earl and Jeanette had given us a nice coal stove, but we had a very difficult time finding coal that would burn. We had not been equipped for this new responsibility, but we did survive.

As in my past years, I did not consciously relate "cold" and "death" as synonymous. However, looking back, these feelings of insecurity were interlinked in my unconscious mind because of our childhood losses. And oh, how I missed Ray and Pauletta, Phil's younger brother and his young bride in Virginia. We had had some great times of visiting as we were all newlyweds. Cooking dinners for each other, going to the same church, and just being there for each other, such fun times.

Where I had had the comfort of an apartment with the heat furnished and with a telephone, I now had neither. The radio did pick up a station where I could listen to some Christian programs each morning, but even with that, Satan began his evil attacks on my mind and emotions. I felt isolated from family and friends and my church family whom I had left in Virginia. The devil loves to attack us at our most vulnerable times.

We did get a telephone some time later, which was little comfort as it was an eight-party line.

After Phil went to work each day, and I had done what little bit of work needed to be done, cleaning, baking cookies, and cooking, I remember just walking from one room to another with my footsteps echoing on that cold, bare hardwood floor. Is there a more awful feeling than being alone and lonely and cold? I had no way of connecting my abandonment as a child to these current feelings of being left alone with seemingly no one available with whom to talk.

Summer finally came, and I loved working in the little vegetable garden our landlord had prepared for us in his own garden spot. The warm sunshine was truly great therapy for me. However, the days were so very long and lonely. We bought a new car that summer, a new Ford Galaxy 500 with a stick shift. As there was now more daylight when Phil got home from work, he began teaching me to drive. I had gotten my driver's license in high school but had never driven a stick shift.

One evening, when Phil had come home from one of his twelve-hour workdays and I was in my depressed hormonal state, I remember asking him, "Have I always been this way? I remember when I used to sing," meaning I sang while working around the house.

He didn't answer me. I was so searching for some relief from my misery. I wanted to be validated. I needed someone to say to me, "You're not crazy. You are going to be okay." But dear Phil didn't quite know how to answer me. I'm so sure he had no idea of just how depressed I was.

Our baby girl, Julie, was born that August. I held her in my arms in the hospital and sobbed out my heart, wondering why we had brought a baby into this awful world. Those were my very thoughts. The only person with whom I shared my heavy heart was an elderly lady who was in the hospital room next to mine. She was a kind listener.

Here I was, with a newborn baby and a wonderful, loving husband. We should have been the happiest family alive, but my world was only dark and cold and lonely. No one could penetrate this dark gloom engulfing me, and I deeply resented anyone attempting to "help" me.

It's amazing the amount of pain and fear one can carry inside and still manage to function as somewhat normal. While life had been manageable while we were in Fairfax County, Virginia, all these sudden changes, hormonal and physical, were whittling away at my sanity. I felt disconnected and distant from others. The least amount of criticism or instruction brought on a fire inside of me. Sometimes I felt so threatened that I had to swallow hard to not let this rage emerge from my mouth, but other times it came out, hurting and wounding those I loved most.

It would be many, many years later in a Christian

counselor's office that I would be introduced to the words "abandonment" and "rejected." I remember saying to him, "You say those words to me, but they mean nothing to me! I feel nothing!"

He was attempting to help me process my childhood losses.

I now have an understanding of two significant events in my life of which I had not been able to explain my response at the time. One had been in Falls Church, at my church where our youth leaders were moving away. On a Sunday evening, my roommate, Sonja, and I had attended their going-away celebration. I remember standing alone against the wall of the large basement room, where everyone was talking and sharing and eating. An overwhelming feeling of loss welled up in my chest. Tears rolled down my face as I attempted to confine my emotions. I felt very embarrassed and never did understand why I had felt such pain. My heart was so heavy.

Another time many years later, I experienced the same feelings of loss when my pastor, whom I deeply respected, left our church to begin his ministry at another church. Only this time I felt intense anger but didn't consciously know why. I simply decided the new pastor in our church would never feel acceptable to me. It was four years before I finally began to accept this change. In both cases, there had been what felt like "abandonment" to me with two very different responses. Though totally unconscious, saying goodbye to an authority figure seemed to create separation anxiety for me.

The devil had convinced me of this lie: "God will take everyone you love."

So here I am, with the heavy responsibility of protecting my baby daughter. My overprotective maternal instinct kicked in, and I became more emotionally controlling than ever before. I remember one evening, when Phil's mom and dad brought Phil's aunts and Grandma Katie to meet our new baby. We were expecting them, but no one will ever know the terror I felt in my heart as I had to allow each one of them to hold my baby. I really wasn't even comfortable with her very own daddy holding her. Talk about a control freak! What absolute craziness ran through my entire being! Demonic spirits must have been my tormentors, adding to my already damaged emotions. Fear truly is a major tool of our archenemy, so opposite of what God has promised his children.

I felt I had no friends, no mother, no one with whom to talk, except Phil's mother, and I was so stubborn about receiving any advice from her or my sister, Jeanette. Even in my emotional state, I was still such a "know-it-all."

Our most common form of communication in

those days was by letter as no one made a long-distance phone call unless it was an emergency. My mother-in-law was able to call me locally as we were only about seventeen miles apart. Even though she always had our best interest at heart, I just didn't want to talk to her. I resented her and felt threatened by her because she would ask questions that could have exposed my awful shameful childhood secrets. No way was I able to share my childhood losses with her. I was many years away from being able to voice them aloud even to myself.

Traveling from our home to Parsons to visit Phil's parents or to see a doctor was a treacherous journey down a mountain called the "17-Mile Mountain." The road, Route 219, was narrow, curvy, and in places, very steep, with wooden guard rails and heavy wire cable strung from one post to the next. Many places the guard rails were hanging in midair as the roadside had washed out beneath them. I was terrified.

The fear of riding down steep, narrow mountain roads and crossing bridges had been an intense fear from my childhood. To me, this was normal, but no one, including my husband, had any clue as to the anxiety I carried inside of me. So one night, as Phil and I were returning home from Parsons to our home in Davis, I must have been suffering from this overwhelming terror of going off the road and rolling down over the side of the mountain to our deaths, so I was telling him how to drive. I surely must have sounded so much more of a nag than I ever realized because he pulled over onto the side of the road and made me drive home. I was shocked at his response, not realizing how my fear had caused me to be so out of control.

When Julie was about a year old, we got a phone call from my aunt Mabel, telling me a more suitable house was available for us to rent if we wanted it. We did. This house was so much more inviting, so we packed up and moved several blocks away. It was comfortable and easier to heat. I felt more content and more able to maintain a somewhat normal way of life for our family. It was in this house that we lived when our son, Bradley, was born.

ooooo

We moved from Davis, West Virginia, to Deer Park, Maryland, in 1968. Bradley was approximately eight months old, and Julie was three. Julie had a difficult time, even for such a little girl, adjusting to our move and for a few days, kept saying, "I want to go home."

And I felt so sad for her and so guilty. After all, I had been the one who had engineered this move because Bradley's pediatrician had told us we needed to move from the house where we lived because of the mold on the walls of one of the bedrooms. He thought this might have been responsible for our baby boy getting the croup so severely. But the move for me meant that we would be closer to a church.

In 1971, Phil had a very serious heart attack. He was thirty-two years old. Once again, I was gripped with immobilizing fear that my husband was going to die. He was hospitalized for an entire month, and later we traveled to Cleveland Clinic just for him to get a heart catheterization. The results from this test revealed he had atherosclerosis or hardening of the arteries.

Phil, Judy, Bradley, Julie

Less than two years later, we moved from Deer Park, Maryland, to Cherry Ridge Road near Mt.

91

Storm, West Virginia, for Phil to be closer to his job. It was this move that compounded my feelings of insecurity and anxiety once again. Life, for me, was reasonably peaceful while we were living in Deer Park, Maryland, but now we were in a new neighborhood and new neighbors.

I was constantly searching for a more intimate relationship with God, but it seemed I just would never measure up to my concept of his expectations. It was unfortunate the church we attended all those years implied our best was never good enough. Just as there had been little or no grace shown to me in my life, this church perpetuated my guilt and feelings of worthlessness.

Each morning I would get up early to cook Phil's breakfast and pack his lunch as he prepared to leave for work. After he was gone, many times I sat down on a chair in the kitchen and stared into space. Once again, I didn't connect these feelings of "nothingness" as depression. I was less than loving to my little children. I remember my Julie, probably seven or eight years old, cautiously peeping around the corner from the living room into the kitchen to see if I was going to welcome her into my arms for a hug. And this was risky for her because when I was in this mental state, seeing her jolted me back into my role of mommy—back to reality.

Eventually, I was able to begin a children's Bible

club in my home after school. My dear friend, Cleda Paugh, had traveled from Oakland, Maryland, to help me get started. God did bless these times in ways unknown to me until one day many years later when I met a young lady who looked familiar as I walked down the sidewalk in Oakland. Cindy had been one of the little girls in my Bible club. She hugged me and said to me, "Every time I hear the song 'Thank You for Giving to the Lord,' I think of you."

Tears rolled down my face. I so much needed that encouragement. Cindy and others had come to know the Lord Jesus as their personal Savior through that Bible club.

My feelings of worthlessness continued, though most people who knew me wouldn't believe this because of my efforts to be in full control of everything. This was a constant battle. I would come to realize many years later that my damaged emotions kept me in near panic mode inwardly. It was an unconscious force that drove me on.

As a young mother, another great fear was that of dying and leaving my children. Therefore, my mind could be quite consumed with any unusual physical ailments I might experience. So once, when Julie and Brad were probably ten and eight years of age, I got up one morning coughing up blood-tinged phlegm—I was terrified. Not telling anyone of my inward panic, not even Phil, I went to the doctor. He had me admitted into the hospital an hour from our home for tests. Knowing my anxiety, I probably convinced him I had cancer. Looking back, because of the frailty of my emotions, I was not able to even have enough mind to see plans were made for the care of my children, but I had left all that up to Phil. I never knew just how he managed to take care of everything at home and still go to work. I was in the hospital for four or five days.

My second night in the hospital, while still being extremely fearful of dying and leaving my family without a mother, I was lying in bed reading my Bible. I turned to the Psalms and read in chapter 128 verse 6 (KJV), "Thou shalt see thy children's children."

What? Can God speak to me in such a manner? Well, yes, he did! As I read those words and then read them again, a sense of peace enveloped my body, soul, and spirit. God gave me assurance that I was not going to die. Having a cold, the blood I had coughed up that morning was that I had probably broken a blood vessel because of such strenuous coughing.

My Phil passed into heaven in January 1981 at age forty-two. I did *unconsciously* what our mother had done when our daddy died. She was home with her children. My two children, ages thirteen and fifteen, were with me at Jeanette's home, which had been my homeplace. In indescribable anguish, on that late cold winter night, I had told goodbye my beloved husband kept alive only by life support in the hospital and went to my sister's house to stay and wait for that call from the hospital. I was able to sleep for a few hours, and early the next morning, the call saying he was gone came. Jeanette and Earl and I were in the kitchen, just talking quietly. I couldn't cry. I was numb. A couple of hours later, when Julie and Brad awoke and came downstairs for breakfast, I had to tell them their daddy was in heaven. Julie started crying, and Brad ran out of the house. I didn't follow him but wondered afterward if he had done the same as my brother, Jimmy, age fifteen, who, when he had found out our dad had died, ran over behind the barn and wailed out his grief. My Bradley was barely thirteen years old.

I have many regrets about the way I was not able to hold and console my children when they lost their father. Having never begun to grieve the losses of my own parents, I had no way of even understanding their grief. I also felt very guilty for many years for not being there in the hospital with Phil for his last hours on this earth. I felt like a coward.

Later that day, choosing to go alone, I returned to the hospital to retrieve Phil's personal belongings. As I drove, I relived the events of those last two or three days: the sudden stroke he had had late in the night which sent him to the hospital in Oakland, seventeen miles from our home. Earlier in the evening, he had helped me with some artwork for my bulletin board at the Christian school where I taught kindergarten and first grade. We had gone to bed and were sleeping. I was awakened by an unusual movement beside me. I jumped out of bed and turned on the light. I ran to his side of the bed and looked at him. He couldn't speak. He grabbed hold of my hand and wouldn't let go. How long had it taken him to get me awake, I would never know. His paralyzed side was next to me in the bed, and he couldn't turn to touch me to get me awake. As I now stood on his side of the bed, his hold on my wrist was so tight that I had to actually wrench my hand loose from his. In a panic, I said, "Let me go! I have to go call an ambulance!"

I ran to the kitchen and called 911. My neighbor, Hilda Cosner, who was an EMT, was at our house in a few minutes. The snow was very deep, and it was extremely cold. Hilda told me months later she didn't think they would ever make it to the ambulance with him, trudging up our driveway through the deep snow.

I had called my friend, Wilda Fitzwater, to tell her we were taking Phil to the hospital. She and her husband met me there when we arrived. Jim and Wilda stayed with me while the doctors worked on him. There was not an empty room in which to put him, so they had put him in the hallway of the hospital. I was not understanding what was being done, and I felt so helpless.

I returned home before our children awoke but noticed that Brad had been up and had his Bible open on the kitchen table where he had been reading it. He told me later that all the people talking had awakened him. It had not occurred to me that one or both of my children might be awake and worrying all alone at home. How frightened he must have been. However, it was comforting to know he had gone to God's Word to seek his own comfort.

Returning to the hospital later that morning, I noticed Phil was in and out of consciousness. I looked down at him, and he would open his eyes and look up at me. Our unspoken words were evident to each other. "I love you so much, and I am so scared."

I did ask him questions, like "Do you have any pain?"

He shook his head "No."

As I wondered if he was getting proper care, I thought of having him transported to Cumberland, Maryland, an hour away, where his doctors were. I called Dr. Fiscus to ask his opinion. He conversed with doctors in Oakland then called me back and said, "I don't think it will make any difference."

He was actually telling me Phil was not going to live no matter what I chose to do, but this very telling statement totally bounced off my conscious thinking. After much turmoil inside of me, I finally made up my mind to have him moved to Cumberland. As they transported him, I can only assume I returned home to get the children and some clothes and took them to the house of my sister Jeanette. I really don't remember. I am glad I did have him transferred to Cumberland. At least they made him comfortable and actually attempted to help him.

As he lay in ICU on a ventilator, I slept some in the waiting room. My brother's wife, Nora Lee, remained with me. Her presence there was so comforting to me. Someone brought Julie and Brad to the hospital, and I asked them if they wanted to see their daddy. One did, and one didn't. I don't remember who went in to see him, but he or she went into his room alone. I didn't go in with him or her. It's obvious to me now as I write this that I had nothing, no rationale, in which to face the reality of this loss. Shock? Denial? I guess only someone trained in this type of trauma could explain my behavior.

It is just so sad that this mother had no way of tuning in to her children's pain. I couldn't comfort them, and I couldn't bear to stay in Phil's room for more than just a few minutes at a time. This loss was just beyond my comprehension. I wanted to run away and scream this wasn't really happening, but I just internalized the pain, lay down in the waiting room, and slept. Sleeping was probably my escape. There has never been another time in my life when I felt so helpless, so wrought with pain and grief.

After processing some of these events on the way to the hospital to reclaim Phil's belongings, I was directed to the department where his few personal belongings were. Still quite emotionally numb, I quietly signed for them and left to return to be with my children.

Earl went with me from Fort Ashby to Oakland to the funeral home to make the arrangements for the funeral. I had no idea what I was doing. When we were taken into the room to pick out a casket, I looked around and said, "That one. He liked blue."

To this day, I don't know if it was a cheap or an expensive one. I was so very thankful to have Earl with me. He had always been the rock that held our family together. He was always willing to help any of us who needed help.

Our first night at home after Phil's funeral, Nora Lee, once again, was there for me. She spent two nights with us. What a comfort she was. I don't remember anything she might have said, but just having her there was wonderful.

The pain of being at home without Phil was more than I could bear, so within two or three days, we got back into our daily routine, traveling the seventeen miles over snowy roads, where Julie and Brad were enrolled and where I taught kindergarten and first grade in our Christian school.

A short while after Phil's death in 1981, I remember one particular night when I was sitting in bed with my Bible on my lap. My heart was breaking. Overwhelmed with my grief, I was crying my heart out to God when I felt such a warm, comforting filling of the Holy Spirit, my Comforter. I remember saying, "God, this is so good. I want all that you have for me."

His comforting love consumed me and wrapped me like a warm blanket. It would be some years later that I would remember the seriousness of this prayer.

My dear mother-in-law, Elsie, said to me shortly after Phil died, "Judy, he was happiest when he was with you."

These words were such a precious comfort to me. He truly did love me with an unconditional love. Elsie also said, whenever she and I would have a disagreement, Phil always sided with me. And I answered, "He shouldn't have," meaning that so many times, she was right.

However, Phil stood by me. She and I had had some stressful episodes together. Elsie was a kind and tenderhearted godly, woman and she seemed to be determined to "mother" me, but I couldn't comprehend her kindness, and I trusted no one, not even her.

Now, sixty-some years later, I'm still verbalizing for the very first time some very painful events/losses that happened to me as a child/young adult. There is such a new openness in my spirit as a result of sharing my life experiences, actually speaking of them aloud with another trusted person.

I continued working at our Christian school, finishing out that year in the classroom and working as church secretary the following fall. It is indeed a very stressful way of life when a person's emotions keep them in a state of anxiety and near panic as they attempt to ignore facing the pain of a tragic loss, such as being widowed. With the gauge on my energy tank being on empty and being so absolutely needy, I ran full speed ahead once again, putting the church activities ahead of my children and our church leaders showing little to no mercy on our circumstances. Though I loved the ladies I worked with at the school, I'm sure I was partly to blame as I wouldn't allow anyone close enough for fear of having to literally face myself. As with my mother-in-law, my lack of trust kept others at arm's length.

I've learned it is so very important to be in a church where the truth is preached and taught with wisdom and compassion. It would be a few years later that I was led from that church into another one, where the teaching nourished my soul.

In the fall of 1981, a man came from his home in Michigan to Maryland to visit his brother who was a member of our church in Oakland. His name was Jim Jackson. His dear wife, Laura, had passed into heaven some time before this. Laura was a sister to my good friend, Cleda Paugh. The next year Jim returned to Oakland to visit his brother, so he said. (*I'm smiling.*) He told me he had met me the previous summer and kept thinking about me. I had not remembered meeting him. I thought it was a joke that he was interested in me as he was twenty years older. However, he had met me at my most vulnerable time in life. I was desperately insecure, and Jim's strong confidence was rather appealing to me. It appeared he could take on any task and conquer it. In the earlier days of having met him, I would laugh inwardly at the absurdity of marrying a man with such an age difference, and the next day I was drawn in by his take-charge personality. He also reminded me somewhat of my dad and my uncle.

Jim had been a medic in World War 2 and was a Pearl Harbor survivor. He had come through more than four years of intense fighting and bloodshed, along with other emotional losses. He had known nothing of the baggage I was carrying into our marriage, and I knew nothing of his.

I learned his mother had passed away while he was in the army and was not allowed to come home for her funeral. When he was discharged from the army, his dad had sold their homeplace, and he had no place to live. He had married his prewar sweetheart shortly after that.

Though Jim was twenty years older than me, we had been brought up with very conservative values of hard work, honesty, integrity, and a healthy or unhealthy fear of God. I now know even an unhealthy fear of God is better than having no fear of God. With no fear of God, the human heart will pretty much become its own conscience, doing "that which is right in his own eyes" and with very painful consequences.

We married in November 1982.

Jim was enormously talented in so many things, loving to play music, singing, carpentry, plumbing, beautiful woodworking, and numerous other gifts. He had remodeled several houses in Michigan.

I had married him for security. He was strong, was a Born Again Christian, and met about all the standards my "approval list" contained. He attended church faithfully, and he was determined to make me his wife. Jim also insisted I quit my job as secretary at the church. Being so busy with my self-inflicted schedule kept me exhausted, so I was most willing to leave my job. Now I am suddenly at home 24/7 with a man I hardly know.

I quickly became aware of Jim's damaged emotions. Along with his many talents and good qualities, there emerged a very jealous spirit, even of the attention I needed to give my children. Being a very controlling person myself, an intense power struggle emerged.

After a brief time of Jim's constant criticism and the condescending manner of his verbal and emotional abuse, I began to communicate to him in a way that was most unpleasant at best. I was very much on the defensive and quickly attempted to try to defend my children and myself. This turned into volatile situations at times.

My fantasy world was crumbling, and very, very slowly, reality was going to become apparent to me. I felt like I was living with an unpredictable volcano.

I was ill-prepared for this rude awakening in our home as Phil and I had really never had a heated argument or talked much about things that needed changed in our home for life to be more organized, etc. As one can imagine, my home was as cluttered as my mind. Struggle as I did, there seemed to be no way for me to keep the house in order; hence, more guilt and feelings of failure.

My controlling, perfectionist personality and the fear of failing God, whom I had felt I could never please, simply kept me from calling it quits on my marriage to Jim. To have gotten a divorce would have seemed to me I was a failure. Quitting was not in my vocabulary.

The differences in Jim's and my interests couldn't have been more different. My world was very small, and my fears and insecurity kept me boxed in with my routine. This was my comfort zone, and I wasn't going to be coerced and prodded out of it very easily.

Jim loved traveling. He had asked me before we were married if I would spend winters with him in Florida after my children left home. I had said yes, thinking I would cross that bridge whenever the time came.

A few months into our marriage, Jim, my children, and I packed up in a little car and headed out to visit his sister in Fort Worth, Texas. What a trip, the better part of three days' travel. I felt like a caged squirrel in the car, but this was the beginning of God using his divine crowbar to pry me loose from my small surroundings. Any time we were in the car, Jim would be seeing the interesting sights and the beautiful scenery, mountains, valleys, fields of farmland, etc., and would say, "Look at all those cattle!" or "Look at those fields of corn," or "Look at that beautiful yard of flowers."

This interrupted my thoughts, which were not really thoughts, just numbed-out emotions, which was pretty much a way of life for me. I felt irritated. I could have ridden in a car for hours and never say a word to anyone. These would be times of solitude and peace in my isolated world. Jim was seeing beauty in life, which, for me, had been obscured.

He also had learned something about life that was

foreign to me. It's good to work hard, and it's good to have times of relaxation and take time to just enjoy life. I guess I was just programmed to work hard. I didn't know how to have fun.

The next year, flying to Arizona for a week, just the two of us, left some great memories for me. Though my heart was at home in West Virginia, I was beginning to see some beautiful country as we did a lot of sightseeing, and my husband was much more pleasant when he had me all to himself.

After spending that first winter in my little house in Mt. Storm, Jim began building a house in Garrett County, Maryland, which was about twenty-five miles from where we were living but much closer to our church and Brad's school.

Julie was in her senior year in high school when Jim and I married. The next fall, she left home to attend college in Pensacola, Florida.

As we moved from "my" house into "his" house, Jim soon let me know that if I "didn't like it, there's the door." His jealousy and periods of rage continued. Even when I shopped for groceries alone, upon arriving home, he raged about me spending the money, even before I began putting the groceries away. I would be in tears. It was one of these times, after he had finished yelling at me, that I heard him say somewhat to himself, "I've got to stop doing this."

I believe he was beginning to see there was

something terribly wrong, but he seemed to be completely helpless to stop the outbursts. It was like something beyond himself had control of him.

My instinctive mother protection of Julie and Brad from Jim's outbursts could turn me into a raging, crazy woman. I truly did attack him physically once when he was verbally abusing Julie and calling her names. Though he could have easily hurt me at that time, he did not lay a hand on me.

It was in this house that our marriage became volatile enough that we realized there could be some physical violence if we didn't get some space between us. We agreed on a legal separation. Up to this point, there had been no physical abuse, and until now, we couldn't imagine that either of us was capable of any such actions.

With the help of a couple of good men from our church, my children and I moved into a rental house in Oakland, Maryland, about five miles from where we lived. Julie had finished her second year of college near Richmond, Virginia, which I had strongly insisted she do. Brad graduated from high school and decided to head out to further his education, becoming an industrial electrician. Julie was now finally able to decide for herself where she wanted to go to school, and both of them were soon gone from home.

Among different little promises from God to my heart before our legal separation, there is one incident that stands out in my mind. I was still a fighter, but there were times when I knew only God could change my circumstances.

One Sunday afternoon, when Julie had been home from college for the weekend, Jim had told me very bluntly I could not take her back to college that evening. It was more than a three-hour drive for me. We knew she had to get back there, and there was no other way for her to return, except for me to drive her there.

I sat in the living room with my Bible on my lap as he raged and threatened. My Bible was open to Psalm 37. Concentrating on the words of this chapter, I silently read, verses 3–7: "Trust in the LORD, and do good; so shalt thou dwell in the land, and verily thou shalt be fed. Delight thyself also in the LORD; and he shall give thee the desires of thine heart. Commit thy way unto the LORD; trust also in him; and he shall bring it to pass. Rest in the LORD, and wait patiently for him ..." (KJV)

I prayed for God to intervene as I felt quite helpless to change the situation. There was nothing I could say or do that would penetrate this man's determination. As I just sat there with Jim standing over me, and after this stand-off continued for what seemed like a couple of hours, I suddenly heard him say, "You can take her back." I looked up at him in disbelief, and the look on his face was startling. He said, "Did I just say that?"

I said, "Yes."

And he said, "You can take her back."

This time he said it on purpose. The previous time, it was simply God using his voice.

It grieves me now that I was considering Jim the "evildoer" in Psalm 37, but it surely did give me hope that God was going to work through our marriage to bring peace to my heart. I wasn't ever thinking about or praying for God to bring honor and glory to himself through it all. I just wanted relief.

I remember once during those first couple of years into my marriage with Jim that God had given me a promise, which read, "The LORD will perfect that which concerns me …," Psalm 138:8a (NKJV).

I claimed that promise for my own. Though I had no idea what God's plans were, I felt somewhat strengthened and encouraged by this truth. To me, it was God's assurance that he "would never leave me nor forsake me," Hebrews 13:5b.

Julie, Brad, and I had about seven peaceful months in our rental home in Oakland before each of them went their separate ways to further their education. After they had left home, Jim asked me to come back to him. I had not had a sense of peace or contentment all those months being separated from him. I knew going back to him was the right thing to do if I wanted to obey God. God was leading, and I was obeying but with a fearful heart.

We soon sold the house where all the sad memories were and purchased a small farm several miles away. There was an old two-story farmhouse as well as several old outbuildings, and I could see Jim had great plans for remodeling the house. He had also taken in to account the quality of the wonderful old wormy chestnut boards from several outbuildings. Removing nails and using his planer to clean them up, the interior of the farmhouse was richly garnished with these beautiful boards. We poured ourselves into tearing down and ripping out old plastered walls, and he began his talented magic on that project. At the same time, we were having a new house built on that property. Though he was still very controlling of me, we worked side by side on this work.

I missed my grown children but had little time to grieve the empty nest syndrome a healthy family might have known, and sad to say, I was relieved they were out of this turmoil and discord.

God was working on me consistently, and I was attempting to obey the instructions given to me by my dear friends, Mr. Bill Foster and his wife, Violet. Their daughter, Lisa, and my Julie were good friends. The Fosters had been solid friends and mentors from the time my dear husband Phil had gone to heaven. Once, when I was sharing with them the awful stress in our home, his brief advice to me was, "God says, 'You will seek me and find me when you search for me with all your heart,'" quoted from Jeremiah 29:13 (NKJV).

God used this time in our new house on Garrett Road to continue the "squeezing" in my life. The more he applied the pressure, using my current circumstances, the more I found myself on my knees, complaining to him about my situation. I was still very fearful of Jim.

I did realize many years after the fact that an emotionally healthy wife would not have been as easily beaten down by his demeanor and criticism. But I perceived it as rejection. During this time, I saw myself as ugly and unworthy as I had during my school days.

By now, the desperation was real. My times of being alone were minimal. However, Jim did spend considerable time in his new garage and workshop, and though it was very close to the house, it gave me time to breathe. But feeling panicky he might come in and catch me journaling my feelings or seeing me talking on the phone kept me very tense and stressed out.

As I think about the stress at the time, I now believe that the limited amount of time alone forced me to spend more concentrated time reading and studying my Bible and to pray.

Within a few years of our marriage, I was having to carry out my promise to my husband that I would spend winters with him in Florida. It was during one of our trips to Florida that God got my attention. I always enjoyed gleaning life lessons from radio talk shows, in which people could call in and ask questions, etc. So this day, as we traveled, we were listening to *Focus on the Family.* Dr. Dobson was interviewing Rich Buhler, the author of a book titled *Pain and Pretending.* As they talked about the contents of this book, I broke down in uncontrollable sobbing. Something he said had triggered a memory hidden deep within my subconscious mind.

God used this event to pry open and begin to expose the intense emotions I had carried all these years. I had no idea why I should have responded to this information the way I did. But the door to my heart had been cracked open just enough for me to realize I was in need of serious help. After arriving at our winter location, I purchased the book and consumed the information therein. It was a major stepping stone to begin my healing.

From this time onward, I was even more desperate to find some relief for my misery. I bought books, called counseling hotlines available from godly sources, and spent time on my knees seeking the face of God. I knew he would be the one to guide me through this dark tunnel to the sunlight at the other end, though when one is in the dark tunnel, there is little thought of even seeing daylight at the other end, just a cry for some kind of relief.

At times God would remain so terribly silent in my searching that was very bewildering and frustrating to me. I remember once, as I had knelt to pray in our bathroom, which was my only place of solitude, with intense emotion, I was crying out my pain and misery to him, "What is wrong with me, Lord? What is wrong with me?"

This was one of his incredibly silent times.

Psalm 42:4 reads, "When I remember these things, I pour out my soul within me" (NKJV).

Dr. John MacArthur says, "These are attempts at trying to unburden oneself from intolerable pain, grief, and agony."

Verse 11 of the same chapter reads, "Why are you cast down, O my soul? … Hope in God" (NKJV).

God was ever so gently using his divine crowbar to lovingly but insistently break up the hardened shell around my heart. Only then could he loosen and begin to break down my self-made fortress, which kept me locked inside and everyone else locked out. I wanted to trust him but as yet did not know that he was fully trustworthy. I totally didn't understand his mercy and grace. He wanted to show me he was not the demanding, unkind God that would take from me everyone I love. In reading the book of Jonah in the Old Testament, I find it interesting, amusing even, that Jonah, though he was extremely angry with God, described God's character as "Ah, LORD, was not this what I said when I was still in my country? ... For I know that You are a gracious and merciful God, slow to anger and abundant in lovingkindness, One who relents from doing harm," Jonah 4:2a, c (NKJV).

I clung to the truth in Isaiah 41:10 (NKJV), which reads, "Fear not, for I am with you. Be not dismayed, for I am your God. I will strengthen you, Yes, I will help you, I will uphold you with My righteous right hand."

God was holding my hand. He was quietly and patiently waiting for me to be ready for his answer. Up to this point, I still thought my husband was the only one to blame for our discord.

Our Heavenly Father is so very loving and patient with his children. He alone knows the pain and turmoil we carry. His loving desire is to set us free. And God is not on a timetable. If our desire is to know him, he will keep bringing us around time after time to the same roadblock until he accomplishes his purpose.

Different times he used the voice of my younger sister, Linda, to get a message to me. Once, when I was complaining about my difficult second marriage to her and our other sister, Jeanette, though she says she didn't remember saying it, her words were, "And Judy thinks it's all Jim's fault."

Another time, she simply gave me a gift, a simple little statue, which read, "Nobody's perfect."

Yes, this also helped open my eyes. Linda's survival mode was making others laugh. She was good at it. There was a time when I felt she should have had her own comedy show on TV. This reminds me of a little poem Linda wrote titled "The Ball of Clay."

> While rolling down the path of life
> We often hit a boulder;
> Not knowing the dent it made
> Until we grow much older.
> We roll off course year after year
> Until God calls us back.
> Sometimes it takes a lifetime to get us
> Back on track.

Linda's personality was that she, unlike me in earlier years, had the ability to actually listen to other people when they talked; and she truly cared about others, even in the midst of her own painful losses and difficult life. All her adult life, Linda has had an immeasurable love and compassion for hurting children.

Many times during the years of God's squeezing me to the end of myself as I struggled to obey him while still not letting go of past trauma, I remember crying out to him in anguish, "God, I don't want to do this anymore!" and even more intensely, "God, I don't want to do this anymore," eventually ending with, "But I will."

I was finding, for every time the warfare or power struggle of my soul brought me to this decision, that is of surrendering my will to him in a very distinct area of my life, he took control of this decision and did for me what I was not able to do for myself. "For it is God who works in you both to will and to do for His good pleasure," Philippians 2:13 (NKJV).

When God put his divine finger of love on a certain issue, stronghold, which had me in bondage, he was never vague in his demand of what that "issue" was. He zeroed in on it in a spectacular way.

ooooo

Living on Garrett Road, I loved walking from our new home to the farmhouse, which we were still in the process of remodeling. It was quiet with no houses nearby. I felt like I could be totally alone to talk to God. It was during one of these solitary treks that I would be able to verbally acknowledge the truth about Daddy's choice to end his life. I said to myself, "That was a terrible thing that my daddy did."

I believe it was that day when I made the choice to forgive him without any emotion. I quietly spoke the words, "God, I choose to forgive my daddy for leaving me."

It was simply a choice to forgive because God says we must forgive those who wrong us. No emotion, no tears. Just a simple choice, a decision. God heard that prayer, and he reminded me later of my choice.

Our lives continued on much as before with my workaholic husband outstripping me in his need to stay busy or contemplating his next project. This sometimes meant we would be selling our home and building or remodeling at a new address. Neither my mind nor steps were able to meet his fast stride. I cooked, made coffee, prepared many meals for our relatives and friends. Jim had two brothers along with their wives living in the Oakland area. We loved inviting them and at times our friends to have dinner with us. Jim became quite proficient in the kitchen, cooking as well as baking pies, cookies, etc.

We were able to remain in our new Garrett Road home for five years. This was my favorite place, and it was the longest time we ever spent at one address. It was at this address where Jehovah Rapha, "The God Who Heals," continued whittling away at my tough exterior protection.

I don't know just when I made the conscious decision to surrender my heart to God, giving him access to every room. Was it that night in January 1981 when sitting alone in my bed with my Bible on my lap, grieving the loss of my husband, when the presence and comfort of the Holy Spirit wrapped me and held me close like a warm blanket? And I said, "God, this is so precious! I want all that you have for me." Was it then, or was it during one of those times several years later as I struggled within?

God had begun his good work in me as a child in 1949, when he had given me the grace to respond to his drawing of my heart to himself and I was born again, saved by the shed blood of our Lord Jesus Christ. I believed. I trusted. And I became a child of God at that moment. It's now April 1989, and my fear of consciously trusting my concept of God was still very shaky. Lies about God the Father had been placed in my young child's heart by the "father of lies," and I carried them through life thus far. The enemy loves to drive a wedge between a child and her trust in God. I refer to this time as my "forty years in the wilderness," though it seems like my wilderness wanderings have been far more than that.

Also, it seems that most of our teaching at church, and from Daddy by his example, was about the wrath and anger of God and not at all balanced with his great love and grace and mercy. When I discovered a footnote written by Dr. John MacArthur about the definition of God's great "mercies," I have returned time after time to the book of Lamentations to try to embrace it, to absorb it, to rest in it. In chapter 3, verses

22–23, it reads, "Through the LORD's mercies[1] we are not consumed, because His compassions fail not. They are new every morning. Great is Your faithfulness" (NKJV).

During the next few years, as God continued his whittling away at my stubborn heart, it was brought to my conscious mind that there were people with whom I needed to ask forgiveness for my attitude toward them. One of them was a mother in our church; I was very jealous of her and her family. My attitude toward her had been less than kind. I, by the leading of the Holy Spirit, was finally able to approach her and asked her forgiveness. Also, God convicted me that I needed to make contact with some people in my past. I asked Jim if he would take me back to Mt. Storm to ask my neighbors, Charles and Hilda Cosner, to forgive me for being such a rude neighbor. Also, on to Davis, West Virginia, where I was able to ask forgiveness to my previous landlady whom I had felt I had treated in a disrespectful manner. In all those cases, they were more than gracious.

"Being confident of this very thing, that He who has begun a good work in you will complete it until the day of Jesus Christ," Philippians 1:6 (NKJV).

---

[1] Mercies is a comprehensive term that encompasses love, grace, mercy, goodness, forgiveness, truth, compassion, and faithfulness.

PART 3

"He Looked beyond My Faults and Saw My Need"

THIS NEXT SECTION OF MY STORY MAY BE VERY shocking to some. However, lest anyone should be too surprised, I need to say many of the psalms have recorded events like this, that of the psalmist expressing his intense anger, being honest with God about the pain and trials of life. The difference is he prayed in humility and ended with praise and worship to a sovereign God.

Continuing to search intently for some relief from the pressure of a very painful, very disappointing marriage, I kept crying out to God to help me. I knew my help had to come from him. I have always known, even in my most intense temper tantrums toward him, he was the only one who could bring some relief to my heart. And I might add, he was the only one who would be patient enough to see me through. He *is* patience, love, and wisdom.

A transformation begins to take place as God, our loving Father, silently but insistently speaks and says, "I love you. Will you allow me to show you the pain you are carrying? Are you going to trust me enough to bring healing to your heart?"

I knew the scriptures. "He heals the brokenhearted and binds up their wounds," Psalm 147:3 (NKJV).

"When my father and my mother forsake me, then the LORD will take care of me," Psalm 27:10 (NKJV); but still, my heart screams, "How can I trust you?! You have taken my most precious loved ones from me! If I release my controls to you … well, I just cannot do that! I am too fearful of what you might do. I cannot trust you!"

And he says, ever so gently, "Trust me."

But walking alone on that country road that day, I screamed at him, "I can't trust you! I can't!" As the rage emerged from the depths of my being, I screamed out to him, "I hate you! I hate you!"

I thought he would surely strike me with lightning but nothing. I stood there in the middle of that country road in Garrett County, far enough away from any houses so no one else could hear me, and screamed these words up to the heavens. Then I waited. Nothing. No lightning strikes, just quiet. I was shocked. I was expecting something, any kind of rebuke from him, but nothing. I had honestly not cared in those few minutes if he had struck me dead. But wow, there was nothing, just quiet. So I screamed out my rage again and again.

This very emotional event began to change my concept of an angry demanding God. He had not struck me dead but allowed me to live even after my intense outburst of anger. This may have also been the beginning of God revealing to me the awful load of internalized pain and anger I had been carrying since I was eight years old and had had no idea of how to free myself from it.

There are no words to express the pain of the family left behind from losing a loved one to suicide. Though death by natural causes is most painful for anyone, it seems to me the grief from those losses pale in comparison to this. Many times I had tried to make myself feel what it must be like to lose a mother, but nothing would surface. I could not comprehend how one might be able to grieve that very significant loss. There has been a small amount of being able to grieve the loss of my mother only after God had brought some healing to my heart for Daddy's death. Even facing the effects of my sexual abuse was down on my list of priorities for healing, but I did work through that loss also.

My prayers began to include, as I continued to cry out to him, "God, I believe. Please help my unbelief!"

If the man who brought his daughter to Jesus to be healed prayed this prayer, then it seemed to me it must be an appropriate prayer. I knew my faith was small.

We had transferred our membership from the previous church to Pleasant View Baptist Church. I loved the verse-by-verse teaching and sound preaching from the Bible by Pastor Marty Herron. However, I probably need to describe a bit of my adjusting to this new atmosphere. Having been used to being very busy in the church, upon our arrival at PVBC, it was like God spoke to me. "Now sit down, be quiet, and let me teach you."

Even as I soaked up the great truths being taught, this was certainly an adjustment for me.

Over his years there, Pastor Marty invited many speakers and Christian teaching groups to speak at our church. These also were rich with spiritual food for my hungry heart. One group that had an eternal impact on my personal life as well as ministering to Jim's and my marriage was "Life Action Ministries" from Buchanan, Michigan. I loved their ministry of music, practical teaching, and especially their free handout sheets, of which I collected many and still refer to them. They are rich with applicable knowledge and wisdom.

Revival services had begun at PVBC in the spring of 1989. On the first night, I attended without Jim. An internal struggle was taking place within my heart. God and the devil were pulling on me, one to freedom and the other to continued bondage.

I had been going through a period of challenging paranoia just before that night in April 1989. It seemed to take all the strength I had just to make myself go to church. Voices speaking to my spirit would whisper to me over and over, "You don't belong here. No one here likes you."

But I didn't tell anyone. I just kept going to church. I had no understanding this is what the Bible refers to as spiritual warfare.

Sitting alone on this night, near the front of our church auditorium, I was mentally and emotionally bewildered. As I had always had the feeling I didn't fit in anywhere, that feeling was more profound than ever on this night. Once again, as I had gotten to the church and was getting out of my car, the mental anguish continued. The almost audible voice, not unlike the voice I had heard when I was eight years old, would say to me over and over in my mind, "Nobody here likes you. Nobody here cares about you."

With tears stinging my eyes and fighting those familiar feelings of worthlessness, I struggled to make myself walk toward the door of the church. I now realize isolation is another tool of the devil to keep us in bondage.

As the special speaker began his message, I began to weep. As I silently cried out, "God, what are you trying to tell me? What is it?" my dad would come to my mind, and I would say silently, "No, God, I can't deal with that. It's too painful."

I wept, I sobbed. I could not stop crying but very consciously attempted to stuff that horrible pain back down to where it had always been. However, when God puts his divine finger on something he wants to remove from our lives, he will bring us to a crisis of the will.

At the end of the church service, I slipped into the nearest prayer room alone, where I continued to weep and cry out my deep pain. Once again, I cried out, "God, what is it? What are you trying to tell me?"

And each time, memories of my dad's suicide came to my mind. The heaviness and grieving pain were almost unbearable. Everything inside of me cried out to just leave this memory buried where it was. I returned home that night, telling no one what was happening to me.

The two days that followed were agony. I couldn't stop crying. I finally called my pastor and asked if he and the evangelist could come and talk with me. My husband had agreed to this. He was probably thinking

I truly needed some help, and I believe, secretly, he was very interested in learning more about how God was working.

I thought I had forgiven my father a couple of years before this, but now God wanted me to begin the healing process of this childhood abandonment. He is Jehovah Rapha, "The God Who heals," and he alone can heal our wounded spirit. That fateful Tuesday in April, a warm and cheery day, God brought me to a crisis of the will. Did I want to continue carrying the load of pain or give it over to him? I made a decision to give it to him. With some help from the wise evangelist, I prayed a prayer of confession for my anger toward Daddy for leaving me. I also released to God the responsibility for Daddy's actions, which led me to confess my anger toward God for allowing this to happen.

My emotions during this prayer—I'm trying to think of an appropriate illustration—were like pulling a large stubborn weed, with long roots growing and wrapped around the roots of your favorite prize vegetable plant, choking the life out of it, out of your beautiful garden. In this case, the "vegetable" was my heart, and I thought it would get pulled out of my body as I struggled through this prayer. But God, the Holy Spirit, controlling everything, helped me, and that day the sun became brighter and the sky bluer. Every emotion in me, aided by the enemy I might add, screamed to not do it. But God, the Holy Spirit, by his grace, continued to empower me to carry this confession to its conclusion. The dark cloud of gloom that had hovered over me for much of my life was gone. I felt like a new person.

I went for a walk later that day, and the phrase "accepted in the beloved" kept going over in my mind. When I returned to the house, I looked up the reference to this scripture. It is found in Ephesians 1:6. For the first time in my life, I began to actually feel accepted of God, and I said to myself, "I'm set free. I'm all better!"

But wait, not so fast! It didn't take long for me to realize this was just the beginning. There were more roots of bitterness that had to be loosened and dug out from around my heart—anger toward several others who, in some way, had abused or, in my eyes, had neglected me, but the one toward my dad was the one all the others had seemed to be attached to.

ooooo

In childhood, I had spent many hours in our garden, pulling stubborn weeds from our vegetables. Many of those weeds were immensely stubborn, but I usually won the battle while using a garden hoe or sometimes my bare hands to dig out the last part of the deep-seated root; hence, the reason for picturing the above illustration.

OOOOO

God wanted my heart to be pure and clean, but I had had no idea of what his goal was. I only knew I wanted to be his obedient child, and it seemed to be much more difficult than I ever imagined.

We sold our house on Garrett Road and had moved into the town of Mt. Lake Park, probably five or six miles away. I missed the walks along that quiet country road, but God, in his perfect wisdom, was not about to let up on dealing with my heart until I would be brought to see what was still down deep inside. Jeremiah 17:9–10a (NKJV) states, "The heart is deceitful above all things and is desperately wicked; who can know it? I, the LORD search the heart …"

I had memorized that scripture but was not yet willing to admit this included *my* heart, sort of self-explanatory.

OOOOO

Eventually, I began going to a Christian counselor. I knew I would need help getting free from these intense emotions. After several trips to his office, little by little, more memories surfaced. He had also asked me to bring in pictures of my family, which I did.

I remember one day I was sitting in his large office, with him behind his desk and I sitting across the room from him. Up to this point, he had known about the childhood losses but with no deep discussion of them. So on this particular day, he said, "Today we are going to talk about your dad."

Me, with that familiar protection mechanism still in place: "I can't do that."

He sat back in his chair, folded his arms, and said, "Then we will just sit here."

After a few moments of silence, knowing I didn't want to waste my money on a worthless session, I spoke. "Okay, but you will have to ask me questions," which he had no trouble doing.

Several times I left his office feeling almost totally removed from reality. My brain felt numb. I would stumble to my car and sit there sobbing, trying to regain my mental stability so I could safely drive myself home.

Living in Mt. Lake Park, our marriage was no better. After the work on this house was finished, Jim made a trip to Michigan for about two weeks to help a family member with a building project. I was so relieved to be able to spend time alone with room to breathe. But then he came back. And life went on. Sometime later he had the opportunity to go on a mission trip to Chile with his previous church friends from Michigan. God used this trip to Chile to begin softening his heart. He came back exhausted but with a more thankful heart. That was a wonderful opportunity for him.

Psalm 42:1 (NKJV): "As the deer pants for the water brooks, so pants my soul for You, O God."

Any hunter will tell you this happens when a deer has been running for a long time. He longs for the cool water from a stream.

When we are so needy in so many ways and still pretend we "have it all together," it's kind of difficult to know what we are searching for the most: human love and acceptance or a knowledge of and a relationship with the Most High God, who, after salvation, is our Heavenly Father.

One day I was on my knees, crying my heart out to the Lord. Jim had left the house, and I thought he would be gone for several hours. I was spewing out to God my animosity toward my husband. However, Jim came back home quite unexpectedly. God spoke to my heart and told me to go face him and tell him I would submit myself to him. No one ever despised that word "submission" more than I. I was born with a fierce spirit of rebellion in my heart. Only God knew the people I had hurt and the damage done in my marriages through this stronghold. This was my conversation with God, or rather His conversation with me, in that moment.

God: "Go tell him you will submit yourself to him."
Me: "No."
God: "Do it now."

I knew I must obey at once. I got off my knees, went into the living room, and said to my husband in seething anger, "I'll submit myself to you, but you will answer to God."

Immediately, even though I had obeyed God in a most ungodly manner, he broke that stronghold in my heart. I felt a new sense of freedom. Did I become a submissive wife instantly? Obviously, I didn't, but the devil couldn't keep me trapped in that particular bondage anymore. For me, submission to any kind of authority has been and will always be a conscious choice every day.

I was allowed to begin a ladies' Sunday school class at Pleasant View Baptist Church. There were many times the Holy Spirit spoke through me, and I loved teaching. The class was growing in numbers. However, sad to say, this wasn't the only thing that grew. The pride in my heart grew as well. Lifted in pride, I was inwardly boasting in a work of God for which I had been only a vessel. Pride is one more stronghold that is a process. Many other events have come along to humble me much and often.

I must say I was the one rewarded as I studied diligently to teach those ladies. Never would I have delved into the Word of God under different circumstances. God was bringing some healing to my heart and was revealing himself to me as I sought hungrily to know him.

I had also begun reading books by Andrew Murray, Tozer, Watchman Nee, and others. I wanted what these writers wrote about—an intimate relationship with God. What is the secret to living a victorious Christian life? This was my constant question, and it seemed to be so unreachable.

Our house in Mt. Lake Park sold quickly, and we were once again moving out into the country, on the opposite side of Oakland. Jim had worked much too hard to get the basement kitchen finished on this house as the new buyers had requested. And we worked to pack up for the move to follow.

With boxes packed and sitting everywhere, Jim ended up in the hospital at Morgantown, an hour from our home, with threatening symptoms of a heart attack. It was February in Garrett County. He had had several episodes of these symptoms before, and it once again appeared this one was from overwork and stress. On one of those nights alone in this house, where there were only paths between boxes, I was alone and once again feeling extremely squeezed, to put it mildly. It's possible that those feelings of abandonment were present. I don't know. I began crying and telling God how frustrated I was. I wasn't just frustrated. I was also downright angry, possibly even a bit hysterical. How in the world were we going to get moved? We had had a deadline for getting out of this house, and it was now narrowing down to the final couple of days.

In desperation, I called the lady from whom we were buying the house, asking her if we might be able to get out of the contract to not have to move. Not such a smart idea, she said "no" and explained why. I then had called our real estate lady to see if there was something we could do to stop this move. She explained, if we broke the contract, they could sue. So okay! Now, what? How in the world was I—note, I, just me—going to pull this off? Thus, the complete meltdown on this cold winter night. All doors that had possibly been a way out had been closed and locked.

I felt so helpless. It seemed, in my life, there was always a way, albeit a very narrow way, in which I could manipulate things to come together on my timetable. Well, in this case, there was no wiggle room; there was not one thing I could do about this situation. I had thought it all depended on me to make things happen.

Well, I cried and wept and had my not-so-small

temper tantrum with God. As you may remember, this was not my first tantrum with him. However, I do believe this one stands out in my mind as him bringing me to a point of me being completely helpless and he was going to allow me to sweat this one out for a while.

"God, this is not funny! What are you doing?"

Well, he never did give me a clue as to his plans. I had to look back years later to see what this lesson was all about. I can now see that many times God never does let us know what he is doing. It's all such a lesson in slow motion of Him engineering circumstances to mature us.

When Jim was released from the hospital, we hired movers to get us moved to our new address. I was always an emotional mess on moving day. As we had always had a piano in the house, I can remember watching people move my beautiful piano onto the truck. I can remember in some previous moves that I'm sure I must have sounded like a crazy woman in my anxiety.

○○○○○

The year 1991 was the fiftieth anniversary of the attack on Pearl Harbor, which had ignited World War 2. It was this time of commemoration that prompted Jim to begin sharing his war experiences. People wanted to hear his as well as the experiences of many other local WW2 veterans. The first was an interview by our local newspaper that wanted to print his story, especially since he had been one of the local soldiers from the Oakland area who had been at Pearl Harbor in December 1941. This was a great opportunity for him to begin a small amount of healing of his PTSD from the war. Though I'm sure he carried many untold stories to his grave, these next few years would be an ongoing release of some of the unconscious trauma he had carried.

Jim joined the Maryland chapter of the Pearl Harbor Survivors Association. For the next ten years, we spent every patriotic holiday, being involved in local parades and Jim giving talks in different towns and area schools.

One adventure during those years was that of Jim and me traveling from Oakland, Maryland, to Rockville, Maryland, in a rainstorm, towing a large float, a replica of the USS *Arizona* Memorial, which Jim had designed and fashioned using the chassis of a mobile home. With a door in the back, one could enter to see large maps showing different locations of the battles in WW2. The float won a ribbon for the Pearl Harbor Survivors Association.

I could see the healing God was doing in Jim's emotions as he shared some of his hair-raising war experiences. He found he needed to forgive people from the war, and he shared these parts of his story also. Forgiving those we had no idea we needed to forgive had brought a greater sense of peace in our hearts and lives.

During those years, God continued working on my heart, patiently bringing to my conscious mind "items" that needed to be removed so His Holy Spirit could have more full control. There is no room for unresolved pain and rejection and the filling of the Holy Spirit at the same time. I truly longed for the "peace that passes all understanding," which God promises to each of his children. At this point, there were still many unresolved issues, one of them being the shame I carried causing me to loathe my life story. It seemed my need to speak of my past was greatly hindered by this shame and guilt.

Realizing the need to begin forgiving my husband, I asked God to show me how this is done. Having begun this process, I simply chose to immediately forgive him for offenses that occurred in the present. Facing my past bitterness and anger toward him would take place later on. So for starters, when I served him a cup of coffee, I would whisper inwardly, "God, I'm serving this coffee as unto you," and I attempted to stay up to date on forgiving current offenses as they happened. This too was a daily choice.

Once, when I had called the counseling line of *Focus on the Family*, they sent me a copy of a book by Dr. Dan Allender titled *The Wounded Heart*. I later discovered Dr. Allender was going to have an all-day seminar in Charlottesville, Virginia, titled "Learning to Love Your Story." I was intrigued and felt the need to pursue the idea of attending. With Jim's okay, I made plans to go. The great information from that seminar eventually led me to work through and overcome some of the great burden of shame and guilt, real and imagined, from my childhood losses. I began to have more courage to speak of many incidents that before had seemed too shameful. Thus, the seed was planted in my heart to share my life story, though it would be many years before that seed would actually take root and begin to grow.

OOOOO

I had heard somewhere of a topic called "The Power of a Secret in a Marriage." Since I had never revealed any of the secrets of my heart to my dear husband, Phil, I had no intentions of ever telling Jim. I had been falsely accused of many ungodly things from him and was not in any way going to risk sharing with him the actual events of my past. However, God once again said, "It's time."

Jim and me. Circa. 2001

Very apprehensively, I sought to obey. As we sat at our dining room table, Jim listened quietly as I shared as much as necessary. He asked me no questions, and this topic was never brought up again. I often wondered if God had completely erased this conversation from his mind.

As Jim's health was deteriorating, he must have been thinking seriously about how I would survive the very cold snowy winters in Garrett County all alone. He had had a heart attack a few years before and sometime later survived an open-heart surgery. So he once again decided to sell our house so we could move away from the cold weather. Without sharing a lot of detail, we searched for a couple of months before we found the house God had saved for us. I had my bucket list for our new home: on a hill with a view, sunshine in the morning, and sunshine in the evening. I also wanted no close neighbors. Through our real estate agent, we signed a contract the same day the house was listed. We knew, as soon as we walked in the door, this was where we were supposed to be. It was in town, in a nice neighborhood, and definitely not on a hill, and I was perfectly contented with God's choice. Amazing!

Jim, once again, jumped in to making some changes that needed to be done to make the house more energy-efficient as well as a few other major things he felt necessary.

After twenty-three years in this marriage, my strong and faithful husband was ushered into heaven. The year was 2006, just seven months after we had moved to our new location. Once again, I was left alone. Even as difficult as our years together had been, I know we did love each other. Adjusting to this loss was a slow and painful process. I turned once again to my Heavenly Father for comfort and strength. Much healing still needed to be done in my spirit, some continuing on from childhood and some from the verbal and emotional abuse in this marriage. I quickly made a settled conscious decision, "I will never again get married!"

I was now living much closer to my homeplace, where my eldest sister still lived. She had been widowed for several years, and her health was failing. She and Earl were married for forty-nine years. My younger sister, Linda, and I worked together to take her to doctor appointments and help meet her numerous needs. Those next seven years taught me more about forgiveness and humility. God had brought me full circle to the same place where my wonderful—turned tumultuous—childhood began and back to my sister, Jeanette, with whom I still had unresolved issues. Again, the Lord brought me to consciously choose to forgive her, and sometime later my emotions caught up with this choice. Some healing took place, followed with me having a more compassionate heart toward her. It was painful watching her life deteriorate.

After suffering symptoms resembling a stroke, Jeanette spent the last year of her life in a nursing home. Her son, Marvin, and Linda and I met at the nursing home almost every week to play music and sing with the residents there. Marvin had inherited a great love of music and like his mother, played the piano beautifully. We have wonderful memories of these times there with Jeanette and the other residents. She spent only a few days in the nursing home for that entire year where one of us was not with her. Also, our lifelong family friend, Myrtle Singhas, who had been such a great help to Mother and our entire family, was already in the same nursing home. She and Jeanette were able to visit each other's room.

As bad as the discord had been in our home as we were growing up, we still were there for one another, talking and laughing and reminiscing. In later years, Jeanette had confessed several times, "I was so mean to you kids."

For her entire life, I don't believe she was ever able to consciously admit Daddy "had done a terrible thing" when he committed suicide.

After Jeanette had been in the nursing home for several months, our brother, Jim, was placed in the same nursing home in the room next door to hers. She was able to use her wheelchair to go visit him. Sad to say, he went to be with the Lord about a week after being admitted there. Jeanette followed him to heaven four months later. The year was 2013.

It's heartbreaking for me to remember about how she felt about herself as I remember her saying once, "Daddy said that I would never amount to anything. Wouldn't he be proud if he saw me today to see that he was right?"

While Daddy possibly made that statement in a joking way, the devil drove that negative statement into her heart. As we were going through things she had kept over the years, we found cards and notes from many friends and family who had written to her, expressing their and our appreciation for her being there for them and for us. How wonderful for her to have finally felt accepted as she was received into heaven. I believe, because of his grace, our Lord said to her, "Well done, my good and faithful servant."

Jeanette had "stayed put" and had kept our family intact. I shudder to think of the added-on pain for us if she had chosen to do otherwise.

Linda recently said, "If it hadn't been for our love of music, there wouldn't have been *any* harmony in our home." She still has her sense of humor.

As the years marched on, I had ample time to spend alone with my Lord, getting to know him on a more intimate basis. He continued to teach me how to forgive past hurts and disappointments. As a loving Heavenly Father/Husband, his desire was to teach me he alone is fully trustworthy.

I don't pretend to understand the deep truths of Romans 8:28–29 (NKJV), "And we know that all things work together for good to those who love God, to those who are the called according to His purpose. For whom He foreknew, He also predestined to be conformed to the image of His Son, that He might be the firstborn among many brethren."

So now I'm now beginning to realize this is a lifelong process. It's kind of a joke to think time will come when I can foolishly say, "I'm all better," only in heaven.

I remember there were impure thoughts that popped into my mind, much of them "bad words" I had learned in childhood. I desperately tried to erase them from my mind and my speaking but without success. At last I cried out to God to take these evil words and thoughts from me. I was reminded again, when I choose to surrender a certain stronghold, i.e., a negative habit, to God, he then begins to work it out in my everyday life. For me, change has been a very slow process. For others, the deliverance may be instantaneous.

Another bit of truth that has helped me in my learning to trust God has been this statement: "Confidence in the Lord is a *purposeful decision*, replacing an *emotional* reaction to one's circumstances," Dr. John MacArthur.

Thinking about the stronghold of fear, it eventually was brought to my conscious mind that fear of anything out of my control was what kept me in near-panic mode much of the time. God caught my attention when I read in my Bible a stunning truth. The King James Version reads that the "fearful … abominable, murderers, sexually immoral, sorcerers … and all liars" were listed together as those who would "have their part in the lake which burns with fire and brimstone," Revelation 21:8.

That word, "fearful," caught my attention. Why did God put a fearful person in the same category such as these? I confessed my sin, that is, my lack of trust in him, and that controlling negative power was broken.

"If we confess our sins, He is faithful and just to forgive us of our sins and to cleanse us from all unrighteousness," 1 John 1:9 (NKJV).

This new freedom has been life-changing as I quickly realized, among other things, I became a more confident driver on the road, though my family might think otherwise. I became more confident in making decisions. From a child, I have been inconsistent, always second-guessing myself, questioning whether my choices were right.

Over the last few years, I am finally able to actually calculate time and plan ahead how much time it will take me to be on time for an appointment. Being late for everything in my life was and has always been a major source of irritation in my home and reaching beyond to friends and extended family as well as causing much anxiety in me. My concept of planning out a time schedule for reaching a certain destination was not even available to me. It wasn't something my damaged emotions had the ability to comprehend. There seemed to be a barrier in my brain; I cannot explain it.

Several scriptural truths have helped me erase, or at least minimize, the crippling effects of my feelings of condemnation and lack of confidence. "There is therefore now no condemnation to those who are in Christ Jesus," Romans 8:1a (NKJV). I have visited this truth many times, attempting to get it immersed into my heart.

At age eighteen, while reading in the book of James, I had read that God tells us to have faith when we ask for wisdom. Ask without doubting. Here is the picture that really caught my attention: God tells us that the one "who doubts is like a wave of the sea driven and tossed by the wind."

I pictured myself as a sailboat on wind-tossed waters, always wavering, unsteady. I felt like I was always being driven by some uncontrollable force, like the wind on a storm-tossed sea. Dr. John MacArthur states it like this: "a billowing, restless sea, moving back and forth with its endless tides, never able to settle."

Gradually, my trust in my faithful Father became a bit stronger. Today I simply marvel at his patience, prodding, and continuous unconditional love guiding me through many challenges. The difficult bumps in the road have all been part of his plan to get my attention so he could prove himself to be my "rock and my fortress and my deliverer; my God, my strength, in whom I will trust," Psalm 18:2a (NKJV).

After my husband's death, though I am so blessed of the Lord and somewhat more peaceful, I am still too sensitive, too insecure. I missed Jim's strong arms around me and the sense of security he had given me. While I had resented him strongly, it was his stubborn "take-charge" personality that had given me what I needed. Though I was convinced I had made a terrible mistake in marrying Jim, I believe God allowed it or worked it into my life for specific purposes. It's amazing that God can take a mentally and emotionally abusive marriage to bring one to their knees so he can begin his wonderful healing of damaged emotions. It worked for me. I am so very thankful for Jim's strong resolve to never quit on our marriage even as I was also committed to it.

I met Gene Williams back in the early 1970s, when he had come to our church to hold vacation Bible school, which my young children, Julie and Brad, attended. His mom and dad had been members of my church. After those years passed, the last time I had seen Gene was very briefly in 1981. The year is now 2016.

I discovered through a family member of his that his wife had passed to her new life in heaven many months before, and I sent him a card. He sent me a Christmas card and also thanked me for my card.

He asked me if he could stop by my house as it was on his way to his daughter's house in Virginia, where he was to spend Christmas. I said, "Yes."

Gene and I lived two hours apart.

On that first visit, Gene gave me a CD of Bible verses, of which he had composed music, and I gave him one single sheet of paper containing "My Morning Prayer" composed by Tom Harmon, an evangelist from Owasso, Michigan. This document has been very beneficial to me, and I have often shared a copy of it with anyone I felt may profit from it.

As Gene was leaving my home that day, he asked if he might stop by on his way back to his home after Christmas. I agreed but with reservations. So on his return trip, he did stop at my house but was met with what he later called "a cool reception." I had been widowed for more than ten years and was intending to stay that way.

I laid the CD aside, not feeling very interested in the content. However, sometime later I decided to listen to it. I thought the musical instrument he had used for accompaniment seemed a little hard to listen to but because of my love of music, was captured by the melody of these scripture verses. I began listening to it more frequently while following along in my Bible, writing down each reference. There were eighty-seven verses on this CD. Gene also told me later God had spoken to his heart as he had begun reading and applying the information on the "Morning Prayer" I had given him.

Gene sent me a friend request on Facebook. By now, I'm becoming very anxious. Many years before this, shortly after the death of my second husband, my sister, Linda, boldly told me, if I ever thought about marrying again, to call her. So I called her and told her of my fears.

Linda: "Well, Judy, who is it?"

Me, with intense anxiety: "Gene Williams!"

Linda: "Judy, you don't have to be afraid of Gene Williams!" (She, as well, had known him from his ministry to her church many years before.)

Me, in near panic-mode: "Linda, you're the one who is supposed to get me out of these situations!"

So much for any help from her, I thought. Since then, we have had many laughs over this brief conversation.

Gene and I began sending text messages then came the phone calls. By the end of January 2017, we were beginning to talk by phone almost every night. Gene was easy to talk to, and we began sharing our past, our guilt, our past failures, and forgiveness, eventually beginning to see there was a need in our hearts where we still needed to forgive others as well as ourselves.

In this new relationship, Gene and I knew we would need to bare our souls with each other so there would be complete honesty between us—no pretense, no deceit. This took a lot of courage for us but was so worth it. This also helped us realize openness and honesty would result in our being accountable to each other, something I had never wanted before. One evening, as I was sharing some painful memories, he said to me, "Don't you think a loving husband could help you?" to which I replied yes. Another time, as I told Gene about a painful episode, he said to me, "I don't believe that you have forgiven that person." He could tell by the tone of my voice when I was telling him of the situation.

I didn't like being confronted with my anger issues but knew he was right. We prayed right then, and I forgave that person again. Eventually, my attitude toward that person changed.

I thoroughly enjoyed talking with Gene; however, my fear of marriage was mounting like a smoldering volcano. I was in near-panic mode and didn't know where to turn. When he began talking marriage, I said to him, "How do you know that this is God's will?" He said he had perfect peace about it.

When I shared my fears with my pastor, Ken Lake, he simply said, with a little humor, "You'd better get close to the Lord."

Without a little humor, I thought, *I thought I was.*

It's funny how we like to think we are more spiritual than we actually are.

One morning, sometime later, I went to the bottom drawer of my file cabinet, where I kept my stationery supplies, to get a new pen. There, lying on the floor, was a pile of papers I was sorting to be filed. Right in front of me were papers from "Life Action Ministries." I love their materials as they are geared to reach to the depths of one's soul if she is ready to receive the truth.

The top of the paper read, "The *Heart* God Revives." Beneath that was this scripture, "The sacrifices of God are a broken spirit; a *broken* and a contrite *heart*, O God, thou wilt not despise," Psalm 51:17 (KJV).

I did not even look at the top of the page, but God directed my eyes to the bottom of the page. Number 14 of the list of two columns read like this:

Proud people keep others at arm's length.

Broken people are willing to risk getting close to others and taking risks of loving intimately.

Once again, I knew God had spoken to me. Suddenly, I saw the truth in these statements. I wept with tears of submission as I allowed God to remove fear from my heart. Little did I know this would be the beginning of an open, honest, loving relationship. Though I didn't realize it then, God was leading us to steps of experiencing marriage much like it was intended it to be.

Gene and I married in the spring of 2017. Pastor Lake took us, as he does every couple he marries, through several weeks of marriage counseling. In this, we saw the selfish mistakes we had made in our previous marriages and, thus, tears of repentance. We didn't want to make the same mistakes.

Gene and me. 2017

I read a small portion of a book Pastor asked me to read. In this, I decided I wanted to make this man happy. That is still my desire. I am happiest when I keep God first and Gene second in my priorities. He has been very supportive and has offered much encouragement as I write my story.

No one has been more astounded than Gene and me at what God has woven into our lives to produce such a comfortable, honest, beautiful relationship.

God has brought me from feeling like a worthless, inferior person to the joy of knowing and feeling I am truly accepted, "accepted in the beloved." What a relief! What joy! In a sense, my journey has been richer because I have been forced to search and seek his face until he has cleared from my blinded spiritual eyes my distorted picture of him to who he truly is.

As God has patiently and lovingly removed layer after layer of pain, anger, rejection, and rage from the depths of my heart, the light of his truth and love and acceptance have found a comforting place to take root and to grow. In my opinion, there is no greater pain in life than rejection. We don't consciously put a name to this emptiness because for most of us, it has been there for so long that it feels normal.

"Acceptance in Christ is the antidote to rejection. Those who experience rejection at the hands of others will learn it as a way of life and continue to be part of the problem. Those who find acceptance in Christ will manifest the kind of joy that will offer hope to a loveless, rejection-filled world."
—Dr. Charles R. Solomon, *The Rejection Syndrome*, p. 140

"The way may be long but my Savior is strong, and He holds my hand."
—Words to a chorus I learned as a child

BOOKS I RECOMMEND

Handbook to Happiness by Dr. Charles R. Solomon

The Rejection Syndrome: The Need for Genuine Love and Acceptance by Dr. Charles R. Solomon

The Ins and Out of Rejection by Dr. Charles R. Solomon

Suicide: An Illicit Lover by John Stevens

The Wounded Heart by Dr. Dan Allender

The Blessings of Brokenness by Dr. Charles Stanley

MY PRAYER OF THANKSGIVING

My gracious Father, how can I praise you enough for your love for me in that you have filled my life with such an amazing, eternal heart of gratitude for your patience in changing me from an empty, broken little girl into one of joy, love, and contentment?

You took that little faith, which you gave me as a child. You drew me to yourself when I was eight years old, and you saved my soul for eternity. Having been assured of going to heaven when I die, you continued to have mercy on me when my life and heart—my mind, will, and emotions—were filled with pain, anger, confusion, and every evil thought that my sinful heart, along with Satan's lies could possibly put within me.

Through those tumultuous teen years, you continued to protect me, even though I don't now remember having given you any or much of my time. You understood when my imagination told me that Jesus was my friend, and I knew he was always with me, but God, the

Father, was not to be trusted. He would take everyone I loved, my wounded heart would remind me.

My image of him was fiercely demanding, and I felt that I could never measure up to his expectations, though God knows I attempted to do this throughout most of my life.

Lies, deceit, pride, rebellion filled my life and kept me from experiencing, hearing, your gentle drawing. With all my heart, I wanted to please you with my life. My love-starved, empty life was looking, searching for something or someone who would fill this longing, and it was you all the time! Oh, how I do praise you, loving Holy Father, for your gracious peace!

Gracious Father, you placed or allowed different people in my life to give me what I needed at different phases of my life. You gave me my precious Phil, my first husband, who was so gentle and kind, and he nurtured my soul, even though I never did share with him about my shameful childhood secrets nor the abuse in my past. He had just known that my parents had died when I was a child. He would hold me close, and I would feel so secure with him.

With Phil being removed from my life, though never from my heart, you gave me Jim, my second husband, whom you used to be the sandpaper, the hammer, and the chisel to begin the refining, purifying process of my life.

Oh, the pain of this process, and oh, your quiet, sovereign determination to not give up on me. I'm eternally grateful that Jim was a stronger, more determined person than I. I needed that. You did miracles in both our lives in those twenty-three years. Thank you again for your patience and love.

Widowed again, you gave me many years to be alone to concentrate on our relationship: yours and mine. More pruning and refining!

Though many times I was lonely, I was quietly determined to remain single until you called me to heaven. However, you had other plans for me.

You tore down my walls of protection so that I might experience the supernatural joy of giving and receiving openness and love from yet my third husband, Gene, whom I love with grateful thanksgiving. I truly believe few marriages experience the honesty and trust, with no fear of rejection or ridicule from each other as does ours. This has not been an easy time of growth for me, but "as iron sharpens iron," Gene and I continue to challenge each other to be genuine and to continue seeking your face daily and to yield our rights in many areas of our lives.

Heavenly Father, you became the eternal Father to me. I had lacked the love and security of an earthly father. I praise you for your perfect, unconditional love and for sending your Son, Jesus Christ, to earth to pay the penalty for all my sins.

I am forgiven, deeply loved, fully pleasing, accepted, and acceptable to you because of Jesus. This has been a fact from the moment I became your child. Thank you, Father, for saving my soul from an eternal hell and for the promise of spending eternity with you in heaven all because Jesus Christ took the punishment for all my sin and sins when he shed his precious blood on that cross.

Amen.

Printed in the United States
by Baker & Taylor Publisher Services